THE OMINOUS OCEAN

THE OMINOUS OCEAN

Rogue Waves, Rip Currents, and Other
Dangers along the Shoreline and in the Sea

GARY GRIGGS

Guilford, Connecticut

SHERIDAN HOUSE

An imprint of Globe Pequot, the trade division of The Rowman & Littlefield Publishing Group, Inc.
4501 Forbes Blvd., Ste. 200
Lanham, MD 20706
www.rowman.com

Distributed by NATIONAL BOOK NETWORK

British Library Cataloguing in Publication Information available

Library of Congress Cataloging-in-Publication Data available
Names: Jensen, KJ, author.
Title: Titans of bass : the tactics, habits, and routines from over 140 of
    the world's best / KJ Jensen.
Description: Guilford, Connecticut : Backbeat Books, 2022. | Includes
    index.
Identifiers: LCCN 2021059267 (print) | LCCN 2021059268 (ebook) | ISBN
    9781493062874 (paperback) | ISBN 9781493062881 (epub)
Subjects: LCSH: Bass guitar—Instruction and study. | Bass guitarists.
Classification: LCC MT599.B4 J48 2022 (print) | LCC MT599.B4 (ebook) |
    DDC 787.87/193—dc23
LC record available at https://lccn.loc.gov/2021059267
LC ebook record available at https://lccn.loc.gov/2021059268

♾️™ The paper used in this publication meets the minimum requirements of American National Standard for Information Sciences—Permanence of Paper for Printed Library Materials, ANSI/NISO Z39.48-1992.

CONTENTS

Preface

Humans have had a long-term love affair with the coast. At least as far back as the 18th century, a strong belief in the healing powers of cold saltwater bathing, even drinking moderate amounts, brought people to the shores of England. Over time, accommodations developed to serve these seasonal visitors as fishing villages gradually expanded to become towns and then cities. Today, eight of the world's largest cities, with a combined population of about 200 million people, are on coasts. With a more moderate climate, greater economic opportunities, and almost endless recreation opportunities, nearly half of the planet's people live within 100 miles of the shoreline, and these numbers continue to increase.

In addition to these permanent residents, there are tens of millions who head to the coast from somewhere else for their holidays and vacations. In August, northern Europeans, who have usually endured a long, cold, and dreary winter, close up shop and flock to the Mediterranean, to the coasts of Spain, France, Italy, or Greece, to enjoy warm weather, the sand, and the sea. In the United States, those living in northern or interior states typically head to the coasts of California, Hawaii, Florida, and the Caribbean. The beaches and coastal waters can get overcrowded, but this hasn't stopped the migration to the shoreline, either as permanent residents or as vacationers. No matter where we live, we seem to just love the coast and the sea.

Walking along the shoreline, laying on the sand, swimming, surfing, paddleboarding, sailing, snorkeling, scuba diving, or any of a number of other ocean activities can rejuvenate our souls and allow us to return to our normal work lives more energized. For months, we eagerly anticipate when we can finally pack for a week or two of coastal vacation. Those fortunate enough to live along the coast can enjoy these opportunities year round, and these activities can become an important part of our coastal lifestyles.

As well as the relaxation, relief from stress, sense of calm, and adventure and exploration that the coast and ocean provide, there are also a few fears, concerns, and potential dangers lurking, which we often read about in the media or think about from time to time. If you let your imagination run wild for a few minutes, there is no end of the potential hazards along the shoreline and at sea that can instill fear in many of us: hurricanes, tsunamis, rip currents, rogue waves, sharks, and jellyfish, to name just a few.

Perhaps as much as any other single event, the 1975 movie *Jaws* still produces fear and anxiety in anyone who has watched it. This fear may ease a bit after a time, but there is still that dread, worry, or anxiety that a shark attack could happen anytime we're in the ocean. Up-to-the-minute news coverage has also provided videos of such disasters as the 2004 earthquake and tsunami in the Indian Ocean, where tourists staying at beach resorts in Thailand filmed the tsunami battering the shoreline and hotels. This footage has made our concerns about hazards along the shoreline or at sea more vivid. The chapters that follow provide some understanding of what goes on along the shoreline and in the ocean. These explanations put these potential threats and dangers in perspective relative to the other risks we face in our everyday lives. And there are plenty of other life-threatening hazards that we don't usually think about the same way as we think about sharks and tsunamis.

Most high risks are those sorts of health issues that we are warned about when we read the obituaries: cancer, heart disease, brain degeneration, stroke, diabetes, and pneumonia, to name a few; now we can add COVID-19, which as of December 2021 had taken 796,000 lives in the United States. Health-related risks combined take about 2 million lives in the United States on average every year. Then there are the accidental deaths: drug overdoses and poisons (67,367 per year); automobile accidents (42,114 per year); guns (39,201 per year); falls (37,558 per year); and drowning (3,700 per year), among others. The National Safety Council reports that cell phone use while driving leads to 1.6 million automobile crashes each year. One out of every four accidents in the United States is caused by texting and driving and results in nearly 390,000 injuries annually. In 2018, 2,841 people died in car crashes linked to distracted driving. These statistics strongly suggest that most Americans—and I don't think we are alone in the United States—simply don't have that much concern about the dangers of texting while driving.

In striking contrast to these numbers, only one person on average dies from an unprovoked shark attack in US coastal waters each year. One person! Globally, four people die on average from unprovoked shark attacks. Considering the hundreds of millions of people around the planet who spend time at the beach and in the water every year, this number doesn't even compare to the World Health Organization's estimate of the 320,000 annual drowning deaths worldwide.

Statistics are one thing, but emotions and fears are something else. Neither sharks nor any other potential shoreline or ocean hazards are pleasant to think about when we are looking forward to relaxation and enjoyment on a nice beach somewhere, and the odds are very small, infinitesimally small, that something will happen to us. However, we should realize that there are dangers in the ocean and along its edge, but relative to the other risks that surround us every day, going to that tropical island for a vacation or spending a day on the beach is pretty darn safe—and important for our emotional well-being. The risks of dying while driving or biking to the beach, or drowning in a rip current, are much greater than being attacked by a shark while swimming or surfing once you arrive.

For more than 50 years, my own education and experience in writing and teaching has focused on the shoreline and the oceans. This book puts into perspective the hazards you might encounter along the shoreline or out at sea because we should be able to enjoy our time in or around the water without unnecessary fear. There is a lot of sensationalism to sort out. From *Jaws* to *Tsunami*, as well as many other videos, TV programs, and books, we are hit with a lot of information that may or may not be accurate or representative of what happens in the ocean. Although it can be easy to make poor decisions or take risks, the ocean and beach are, overall, extremely safe places to be.

This book covers global hazards along shorelines and in the ocean. While the recognized big-wave surfing spots are somewhat limited in their geographic distribution, rip currents and sneaker waves can occur along virtually any coastline. Rip currents, wherever they might be encountered, take the lives of many innocent but unaware people every year. Tsunamis are mostly concentrated around the Pacific Ocean, with far fewer incidents in the Indian and Atlantic Oceans. Many potentially dangerous ocean creatures tend to prefer warmer tropical or subtropical waters, but there also are others—sharks, jellyfish, lionfish, cone snails, and stingrays—that either frequent or have migrated into more temperate latitudes. So it isn't uncommon to have a chance encounter with any of these beasts in Florida, southern California, the Mediterranean, Japan, and even South Africa and New Zealand.

Chapters 2 and 3 focus on those recreational activities where we intentionally or unknowingly may put ourselves in harm's way or take chances in potentially dangerous situations. These don't sound as frightening as the threat posed by a tsunami, for example, but a surprisingly large number of fatalities occur along shorelines very year, as unsuspecting people are caught in dangerous situations involving large waves. In just 4 weeks of the winter of 2020–2021, 10 people died in northern California after being swept off rocks, jetties, or the beach by large waves.

Chapter 4 focuses on some of the most dangerous sea creatures we may encounter in coastal waters. In most cases, with some knowledge of what these animals look like and a healthy degree of caution, we can safely avoid them. Many of these denizens of the deep and shallow typically inhabit tropical or subtropical latitudes, places where many of us may never set foot in the water, but there are others that you can encounter in more temperate waters. So, while the opportunity to get bitten or stung certainly exists in the tropical Pacific or Indian Oceans, knowing what potentially dangerous creatures may be in residence at your planned vacation site can help ensure that you and your family and friends remain vigilant and safe. On the positive side, none of these creatures are known to attack people.

We then move offshore for chapter 5 on rogue waves and things that on occasion can wreak havoc on even very large ships. Large waves can have major impacts under the right set of conditions. The mysterious Bermuda Triangle, where it seems ships and planes go to disappear, is treated in chapter 6, where I dispel a lot of legends and unsupported stories. Large-scale natural hazards or events that we have absolutely no control over are covered in chapters 7 and 8. These disasters can be devastating to coastal cities and communities, such as Hurricane Katrina in New Orleans in 2005, the massive earthquake and tsunami in Japan in 2011, and Super Typhoon Yolanda in the Philippines in 2013. These events can produce both massive property damage and large numbers of fatalities, but in most cases, we now have warning systems for these events so that we have time to evacuate to a safer place. We can't move cities or communities, but we can save human lives.

There are many things we do in our everyday lives that present far greater dangers to us as individuals than those hazards we may be exposed to along the shoreline or in the ocean. This book explains these natural processes, events, and creatures; why and where they may occur; and what should or shouldn't concern us to provide a clearer understanding of just how our oceans behave. The oceans cover 71 percent of the planet's surface, and that amount is increasing as ice melts and seawater warms and expands. We all ought to know more about that 71 percent for our own well-being, decision making, and enjoyment.

CHAPTER ONE

Introduction

Personal Brushes with Danger in the Sea

GREAT WHITE SHARKS, STINGRAYS, LIONFISH, RIP CURRENTS AND sneaker waves, hurricanes and cyclones, tsunamis, ship collisions, rogue waves—there is no end of things to be frightened of as you step into or sail in the ocean.

During my freshman year at the University of California, Santa Barbara, my roommate Clark and I had quickly become good friends. We were the only guys who surfed in our small, former Marine Corps barracks dormitory at UCSB. We also came from the same geographic area of Southern California. Somehow, the questionnaire they had given to freshman to match up roommates based on lifestyle had worked out in our case.

Clark had an old, balsawood surfboard that had seen the ravages of time. Because it was so waterlogged from years of use, it was half-submerged when he took it on the water. It was more like a log than the ultralight boards of today, which made paddling into a wave and surfing considerably more difficult. At more than 10 feet long, it also weighed a ton, so carrying it around required substantial effort.

On a beautiful, warm September afternoon, I returned to my dorm room to find Clark huddled under a blanket, shaking. I found this a bit surprising on a sunny fall day, so I asked him what was going on. I slowly coaxed the story out of him. He had been out paddling in the kelp beds off Isla Vista, just west of the university campus. Clark was also a scuba diver, so he had a keen interest in just about anything moving in the ocean. He was a few hundred yards offshore that afternoon when he saw a dark shape that he thought was probably a seal or sea lion. Ever curious, he paddled slowly over to investigate. When he looked down, what he saw sent him into a mild shock. Instead of a seal, he saw a large shark directly beneath him. And his board, partly submerged, was just grazing the top of the shark's body. No matter how many years you have spent in the ocean and how macho you may feel, this is not a positive situation for anyone. And I wouldn't describe Clark as a macho guy.

When downed pilots found themselves in shark-infested waters, some advice they were given was to do a relaxed breaststroke toward safety so as not to agitate the water and attract attention. My roommate made it to the beach, but from his condition when I saw him, I don't think he was calm or relaxed as he paddled back with his old, partially submerged balsa board.

In all my years in the ocean, I have never once had any experience remotely close to what Clark had that afternoon. But like 99 percent of us, encountering a shark in the water is one of those things I would just as soon avoid. A shark attack to a swimmer, surfer, paddler, kayaker, or skin diver is something most of us instinctively fear. Horror fiction and films like *Jaws* have tapped into this fear while undoubtedly feeding it further. While all of the roughly 375 shark species worldwide are carnivores, none has any personal agenda against humans, although occasionally sharks will mistake a person for prey. And if you are underwater, as sharks usually are, and you look up at the outline of a surfboard, it could easily be mistaken for a large sea lion or seal.

Two years after Clark's encounter with the shark, I was working out with regular ocean swims along the same stretch of the Isla Vista shoreline where he had his close encounter. I was training for the state lifeguard ocean swim test to be held in May 1963 in Carpinteria, getting ready for the summer beach season. The state beaches in California take only the strongest swimmers, and while I wasn't even remotely close to the pre-Olympic high school and college swimmers in the area, I thought, "Why not give it a try?" It would be a whole lot more enjoyable than working in sweatshop factories, as I had the two previous summers.

It was a typical cool, foggy April morning, and wearing only Speedos, I was just beyond the breaker zone, swimming parallel to the beach, when I felt my hand touch something that wasn't water. I didn't have swim goggles, which weren't commonly used at that time, so my eyes were usually closed. The visibility along this part of the California coast is pretty poor, and with no goggles, I had no idea what was under me in the dark ocean below. With a fertile imagination and a healthy amount of fear, I had little indication of what might have been in front of me but guessed it could be lots of things—and a few that could actually do some damage. My first thought was one of fear: "Oh crap, it's a shark or hungry sea lion." And Clark's close encounter surged into my mind quickly. Fortunately, I had only encountered the edge of a large kelp bed, so I managed to survive my first brush with a near-death ocean experience. But it was still enough to put some fear into my entire body.

It's probably safe to say that most beachgoers fear a shark attack more than any other single hazard at the beach (see figure 1.1). So what are the odds? How often do sharks attack people? There are lots of interesting

Figure 1.1. Great white shark.
COURTESY OF T. GOSS, CC BY SA 3.0 VIA WIKIMEDIA COMMONS.

statistics to provide some perspective and hopefully some peace of mind. Less than one person is killed each year on average by an unprovoked shark in all US waters. You're 25 times more likely to be killed by a dog bite than a shark and 50 times more likely to be killed by lightning or from a wasp, hornet, or bee sting. But very few of us worry about these much higher risks.

While about four people globally die every year from shark attacks, people around the world kill an estimated 50 million sharks each year, primarily for their fins to use in very expensive shark-fin soup. As a result, some shark species are now on the verge of extinction. Doesn't seem quite fair, does it? For those who are brave enough to go to the beach and enter the water, the chance of being attacked by a shark is about 1 in 11.5 million, and a person's chance of getting killed by a shark is less than 1 in 264 million. While I'm not a gambler, I would say these are pretty good odds and they don't keep me out of the ocean. Still, most people are simply frightened to death of being attacked or eaten by a shark. While we are worrying about a shark getting us, 3,700 people are drowning in the United States every year—about 10 every day.

Growing up, I spent a lot of time surfing, paddle boarding, and swimming in rivers, lakes, and the ocean. I even worked as a beach lifeguard in Santa Barbara one summer. As a result, I have always felt that swimming was something that everyone learned to do, sort of like riding a bicycle. From time to time, though, I'll meet someone who never learned to swim or even has a fear of the ocean or deep water. In fact, about 37 percent of US adults can't swim farther than the length of a standard pool. Studies have also shown that, not surprisingly, the biggest risk factor for drowning is not knowing how to swim, which brings up the question, Why don't more Americans know how to swim?

One reason could be a fear of water, which is a surprisingly common trait in the US population. According to a 1998 Gallup poll, 68 percent of Americans (2 out of every 3 people) are afraid of deep, open water, while 32 percent fear putting their head beneath the water, and 46 percent (almost half) fear the deep end of swimming pools. As a lifelong ocean person, I was surprised to discover that there was even a word (aquaphobia) for those people who are afraid of the water. This fear can come from a traumatic experience or even watching a frightening movie like *Jaws*. A fear of water can also be passed down from parents to children, and if a parent doesn't know how to swim, there is only a 13 percent chance that their child will learn to swim. This simple statistic helps explain why many people have an understandable fear of the sea.

Chapter Two

Rip Currents, Sneaker Waves, and Other Ways to Drown at the Beach

Let's be clear up front: Almost everyone loves a day at the beach, whether swimming, surfing, walking, jogging, or just laying out in the sun. While many of us living close to the coast spent the better part of the summers in our youth trying to get a tan, we now know that this is unfortunately a good recipe for skin cancer. These days, most people liberally apply one of a hundred different brands of high-SPF sunscreen to ward off skin cancer.

Melanoma aside, spending time at the beach is probably one of the safest things in life that we can do. Looking at the odds, the drive to the beach on a crowded highway with everyone else racing in the same direction on a hot July weekend is a far more dangerous activity than being on the beach itself or in the water. Once you get to the beach, however, here are some common hazards that you can avoid with a little awareness and common sense, which are unfortunately often in short supply when you are having a good time with friends.

Rip Currents

Rip currents (often called riptides, even though they have nothing to do with the tides) are a common danger at the beach. Australia, like California and Florida, is well known to both locals and visitors for its beaches. A recent study down under found that rip currents over a 7-year period took more lives on Australian beaches (21) than the combined fatalities from cyclones, bushfires, floods, and sharks (19). As there must be a witness to a rip-current death to confirm this cause of the fatality, the reported figure of 21 deaths is believed to be conservative. And there are those who disappear or drown in the ocean, and we don't know what happened. On some beaches, however, being caught in and then carried offshore in a rip current is a good bet. Estimates are that about 4.2 million Australians (1 in 4 aged 16 to 69) have, at least once in their lives, been caught in a rip current. One likely victim who received worldwide media coverage was Australia's former prime minister.

On Sunday, December 17, 1967, Harold Holt, then prime minister of Australia, disappeared while swimming at Cheviot Bay on the Victoria coast, not far from where he had a beach house (see figure 2.1). Although there were many rumors and theories about his disappearance, the final conclusion was that he had drowned. Holt was an active outdoorsman and loved spearfishing, which was his favorite vacation activity and something that he had been doing for many years. He found scuba tanks burdensome, so he preferred to either snorkel or just free dive. Friends said that because of his many hours in the water, "he had incredible power of endurance underwater," and during long parliamentary debates, he sometimes amused himself by seeing how long he could hold his breath. Although he was reportedly able to tread water for long periods of time, he was also described as not a strong surface swimmer.

Holt was just 59 years old and had been in relatively good health throughout his life, although there was a family history of early death. Three months before his disappearance, he had started treatment for a painful shoulder injury and was prescribed painkillers. A doctor examined him just a few days before his disappearance and recommended that he avoid overexerting himself and cut back on swimming and tennis. He had been prescribed morphine, and some thought that his judgment on the day he died may have been clouded by the drug, although there is no direct evidence that he had taken the painkiller that day.

The prime minister had a busy weekend with events and friends, and on the return to his beach house, he suggested that they stop at Cheviot Beach for a swim. It was about 12:15 p.m., and he wanted to cool down

Figure 2.1.   Australian prime minister Harold Holt entering the water at Portsea to go spearfishing in 1966.

and work up an appetite before lunch. He knew the beach well and had swum there frequently. Holt didn't hesitate to get into the water, despite what was described as a "large swell and visible currents and eddies," which may well have been rip currents. One other man in the group also entered the water but stayed close to shore and said he felt a strong undertow even there. Holt swam out into deeper water and was dragged out to sea. While his friends called out to him, he didn't raise his arms or cry for help. He soon slipped beneath the water and out of sight. Despite a massive search, the prime minister's body was never found.

Holt's biographer concluded that "there could never realistically be much doubt that Harold Holt had drowned and, despite being the Prime Minister, he was just one of a number of Australians who drown each year through poor judgement or bad luck." He likely misjudged his own swimming ability and the condition of the ocean that afternoon and was simply overcome by exhaustion (very likely from getting caught in a rip current—one of those "visible currents and eddies"). Alternatively, he could have suffered a heart attack, been stung by a jellyfish, or attacked by a shark.

Despite the continued use of the word *riptide*, rip currents are not at all related to tides. Rip currents are strong, narrow currents of water that move from the shoreline offshore and are actually quite common. They flow more quickly than any human can swim, and the most common response of someone unfamiliar with shoreline currents is to panic or try to swim back to the beach, directly against the current—both of which are bad ideas that can prove fatal. On Australia's roughly 11,000 mainland beaches, an estimated 17,500 rip currents may be present at any given time. In a word, they are quite abundant.

Rip currents can form along almost any beach and typically develop when several large waves break over a relatively short period of time. As the breaking waves continue to push water toward the shoreline, an escape route or release valve where that water can return offshore develops. This is when rip currents can form. They often are evenly spaced along a shoreline and can flow hundreds of feet offshore until they finally dissipate (see figure 2.2). Why they form in the locations they do isn't completely clear, but it may be related to the characteristics of the

Figure 2.2.   A group of rip currents (designated by arrows) along the southern shoreline of Monterey Bay, California.
COURTESY OF DEEPIKA SHRESTHA ROSS © 2012.

breaking waves and bottom topography. Usually visible from a bluff top or slightly higher elevation, rip currents transport suspended sand as they move offshore, creating a plume of discolored water (see figure 2.3).

While these common currents are a significant hazard in Australia, in the United States, they are responsible for approximately 100 to 150 deaths every year. In Florida, for example, more people die annually in rip currents than in thunderstorms, hurricanes, and tornadoes combined. These seaward flows of water are the number one concern for lifeguards on virtually all beaches, and about 80 percent of lifeguard rescues involve rips, some 30,000 rescues a year.

For a weak swimmer, being carried swiftly offshore can be very frightening and can easily lead to panic and then drowning. Though it's difficult to convince a person not to panic when you suddenly find yourself 500 feet offshore, there is another approach. While you can't swim

Figure 2.3. A rip current can usually be recognized from the bluff top.
COURTESY OF DAVID B. CLARK © 2012.

directly against the rip current, the best approach is to swim to one side or the other of this flow to avoid getting carried even further offshore.

On a warm, sunny summer afternoon at a southern California beach (Zuma County Beach near Malibu, to be exact), my brothers, a small group of friends, and I were body surfing and enjoying the waves, completely oblivious to rip currents. In fact, none of us had even heard of them before. I was about 13 years old at the time, and I don't recall warning signs posted in those days. If there were, we completely missed them. At one point, I remember looking around and noticing that we were all a lot further offshore than where we had been a few minutes earlier—maybe 400 to 500 feet from the beach, well beyond where we could touch the bottom. Fortunately, rip currents don't extend very far and usually dissipate pretty quickly. The water was warm, and it was a nice day, so before long, we just started swimming back to the beach, somewhat oblivious of what just happened.

Many beaches today that have frequent rip currents are posted with caution signs, and in most urban areas, there are lifeguards on duty, at

Figure 2.4.   A rip-current warning sign and ways to swim away from the rip.
COURTESY OF THE NATIONAL OCEANIC AND ATMOSPHERIC ADMINISTRATION.

least in the busy summer months (see figure 2.4). Knowing your swimming skills, understanding your surroundings, and making some observations before getting into the water are good precautions. Drownings and deaths arise in rip currents when people are poor swimmers or the water is very cold. In the few minutes that they are being transported away from safety and comfort of a shallow bottom, people panic. Some awareness about the ocean conditions around you is important, and common sense is a wonderful and worthwhile skill to cultivate.

SNEAKER OR SLEEPER WAVES

In recent years, a new name has been given to certain waves that tend to surprise beachgoers: a "sneaker wave," or in Australia a "sleeper wave." The first time I heard this on a coastal weather forecast for weekend beachgoers ("Watch for sneaker waves today"), I thought perhaps I had missed an important lecture in my physical oceanography class in graduate school. This surprised me because I thought I had paid close attention in this class. There were long-period and short-period waves, deep-water and shallow-water waves, spilling and plunging waves, but in going back through my textbooks and meticulous notes, not a word about sneaker or sleeper waves.

The message in the media seems to be that there is a wave conspiracy on the coast. When a group of naïve beach visitors insist on walking, playing, or taking photographs standing at the water line, a wave will sneak up, grab them, and drag them out into the ocean. Waves typically come in sets: A number of smaller waves will be followed by a group of larger waves. These larger waves will wash farther up on the beach, sometimes much further than the previous waves, soaking or removing your towel, blanket, lunch, phone, or camera. And if the water is more than 2 or 3 feet deep, they can overtake and carry young, old, and anyone in between out into the surf zone. Drowning becomes a distinct possibility if a person is very young, very old, or doesn't know how to swim. Calling these "sneaker waves" is a good example of anthropomorphizing a totally innocent wave, simply doing what most waves do and ending their relatively short lives by breaking on the shoreline.

The waves we see breaking on our favorite beach have typically formed hundreds or even thousands of miles away, where a storm and strong winds have transmitted some of their energy to disrupting the sea surface. Just like you can create small ripples or waves in your cup of hot tea or coffee by blowing to cool it down, the wind accomplishes the same thing but on a much larger scale on the sea surface. The longer the wind blows, the higher the velocity of the wind, and the greater the distance of ocean surface the wind covers, the larger the waves can become. These newly formed waves will begin to move out away from their area of formation and can travel great distances before arriving at some shoreline or beach.

Years of observations and measurements in shallow water and at the shoreline have shown that waves often come in sets: an interval of smaller waves followed by a period of larger waves, the ones that all the surfers in the water are waiting for. Most of the time, there will be waves from several distant storms arriving from different directions and converging on the beach at the same time. These could be storm waves from thousands of miles away and others from only a few hundred miles distant. As these different groups of waves arrive at the shoreline, they begin to interact. Depending on the wave lengths of these different groups of waves (wavelength being the distance between two successive peaks or troughs), there may be an alignment, or what we call *constructive interference*, when the peaks from these different wave groups come together to create several larger-than-normal waves, or a *set* to surfers. This will be followed by a period when the peaks or crests of one group of waves coincide with the low points or troughs of another group. This is known as *destructive interference*, and we get an interval of smaller waves (see figure 2.5).

Because there is essentially an infinite number of possible waves that may meet or converge on any beach on any day, the combination of wave heights is essentially endless. We may see sets of four or five large waves or eight or ten large waves, and despite what you may have read or heard, there is no scientific basis for the seventh or ninth wave being the largest. It's just not true. However, given the right combination of wave crests converging or reinforcing each other, we can see a much larger wave or several larger waves breaking from time to time. When this happens at a high tide, the uprush from those large breaking waves can wash much further up the beach and reach higher elevations than the recently broken waves we have not really been paying much attention to.

These are what are often referred to as sneaker waves. These waves catch unsuspecting children building castles in the wet sand and adults who are thinking about things other than constructive interference of

Figure 2.5. Waves approaching and beginning to break on the beach. Offshore, there are intervals of larger or higher waves and lower waves resulting from wave interference.
COURTESY OF GARY GRIGGS.

waves and knock them off balance or wash them off their feet. There is no specific definition of a sneaker wave, nor can their arrival be predicted. These are simply larger waves than are typical for that beach at that time, and they can surprise anyone not aware of their surroundings. Beach weather reports and signs along the California, Oregon, and Washington coasts now frequently warn people to "watch for sneaker waves" (see figure 2.6). There is no geographic restriction to these waves, however; even tourists in Iceland have been caught by very cold sneaker waves (see figure 2.7).

These large waves that wash higher up on the shoreline than many beachgoers expect can also damage homes and other development on the back beach. On July 6, 2020, during a high tide, a swell with very large waves impacted the southern California coast. In Newport Beach, on a

Figure 2.6.   Sneaker wave warning sign.

Figure 2.7.   Sneaker wave at Djúpalónssandur, Iceland.

very low-lying sand spit in Orange County, the combination of the high tide and large waves washed across the beach, over a low seawall, through a beach parking lot, and then into the residential neighborhood. Streets, parking lots, and garages were filled with sand and debris, and cars were flooded. These incidents are becoming more common as sea levels continue to rise but are more hazardous to shoreline property and vehicles than to human lives.

DROWNING

Although many of us instinctively fear being attacked by a shark while in the water, as mentioned earlier, the odds of dying from a shark in US waters are extremely low. However, in an average year, 3,700 people drown in the United States. This is equivalent to 10 people every day. Globally, the estimated annual drowning deaths reaches more than 300,000, making it the third-leading cause of unintentional death worldwide.

To put this in some perspective, the United States Lifesaving Association (USLA) looked at the last 10 years of reports from lifeguard agencies and compared the estimated beach attendance to the number of drownings on beaches protected by lifeguards. Between 2014 and 2018, there were on average about 368 million beach visits annually; 88,000 rescues; and 140 drownings, with 86 percent of these taking place on beaches without lifeguards. The USLA calculated that the chance of a person drowning at a beach protected by USLA-affiliated lifeguards is 1 in 18 million, a really low number.

There are certainly lots of bodies of water a person could drown in besides the ocean, and for those people who are not swimmers or perhaps not very strong or confident swimmers or are small children, the ocean does provide some additional challenges beyond a backyard swimming pool. Most important, waves come in nearly constantly, which can produce a lot of surprises for those unfamiliar with the ocean. Small waves followed by large waves; steep beaches where the backwash can be very strong and pull you down the beach into the next incoming wave; offshore bars and troughs where you may be surprised by stepping into water a few feet deeper. Any of these can surprise someone visiting a beach for the first time. These are all in addition to rip currents and sneaker waves.

Your odds of drowning at the beach are very low, but being in the wrong place at the wrong time, not being aware of your surroundings, or being overly confident in your swimming ability are all recipes for potential disasters during an otherwise nice day at the beach.

CHAPTER THREE

Surfing and Other Water Sports

BOARD AND BODY SURFING

THERE ARE AN ESTIMATED 35–40 MILLION PEOPLE AROUND THE WORLD who surf. And like many other activities at the beach, surfing is an extremely safe sport. As in any sport, however, there will always be a small group of athletes who push the limits: skiing or snowboarding impossibly steep slopes; using batwings to jump and then glide off towers, bridges, and canyon walls; descending without scuba gear to depths that the rest of us wouldn't even contemplate. And then there is the small group of people who focus much of their lives on surfing the world's largest waves. The locations where oceanographic and bathymetric conditions produce massive waves under the right conditions are well known to this cadre of extreme surfers and are sites of celebrated and eagerly anticipated contests: Mavericks near Half Moon Bay, Nelscott Reef on the northern Oregon coast, Jaws on Maui, and Cape Nazaré in Portugal (see figure 3.1), to name some of the better-known spots.

And then there is the subsequent challenge of trying to determine the actual height of the highest wave ridden each year—or the highest wave ever ridden, period. To date, the honor remains with Brazilian surfer Rodrigo Koxa at Cape Nazaré, Portugal, who rode an 80-foot wave on November 8, 2017. While difficult to measure waves this high, Rodrigo is given credit for surpassing the previous record of 78 feet, also at Nazaré, 6 years earlier by Garrett McNamara. Not to be outdone by the men in this arena, Maya Gabeira of Brazil was seriously injured following a

Figure 3.1.   Surfing a very large wave at Cape Nazaré, Portugal.

wipeout at Nazaré in 2013 and returned in 2020 to ride a 73.5-foot wave, the highest ridden that year by anyone and the highest ever ridden by a woman ever (see figures 3.2 and 3.3). Aside from the Rodrigo Koxas, Garrett McNamaras, and Maya Gabeiras of the surfing world, there is a list of tragedies when things go horribly wrong, which can happen quickly. This is not a sport for novices or the unprepared.

Jeff Clark had grown up in central California's Half Moon Bay, watching the waves at Mavericks from his local high school and nearby Pillar Point (see figure 3.4). While it was originally thought to be simply too dangerous to surf, in 1975, when Jeff was just 17 and with the waves reaching nearly 25 feet, he paddled out alone and caught a number of large waves, becoming the first person documented to tackle the waves head on.

In December 1994, almost 20 years later, with huge swells breaking, a group of Hawaiian big-wave riders arrived to surf Mavericks. On December 23, Mark Foo, one of those men from Hawaii, lost his life after

Figure 3.2.   Maya Gabeira.
COURTESY OF ANA CATARINA TELES © 2021.

Figure 3.3.   Maya Gabeira surfing at Nazaré, Portugal.
COURTESY OF ANA CATARINA TELES © 2021.

Figure 3.4. Russell Smith on a large wave at Mavericks, central California.
COURTESY OF SHMUEL THAYER © 2011.

falling forward and wiping out at the bottom of an 18-foot wave—not really big by Mavericks' standards. It was never clear what happened to Mark, but many felt that his leash had gotten tangled in the rocks on the seafloor, and the breaking wave held him down and kept him from releasing himself from his board. When his body was recovered 2 hours later, it was still tied to the broken tail of his board. His was the first death at a location that had become a magnet for big-wave surfers.

Mark Foo had been described as the Joe Montana of big waves. He was mister everything: a media broadcaster, author, businessman, health enthusiast, and traveler. He rode waves for the same reason rock climbers climb mountains: because they were there. He heard about Mavericks and had to see it for himself. Ultimately, his tragic death became a symbol for the lore and legend of this break and also brought worldwide attention to this tiny spot of cold California ocean over a ragged area of seafloor that produces massive waves under just the right conditions (see figure 3.5).

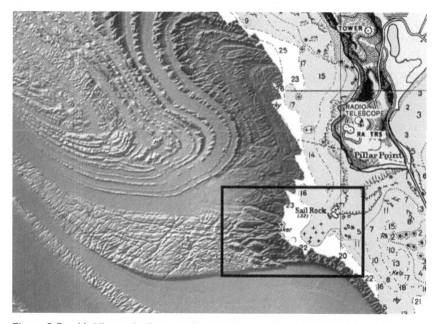

Figure 3.5.   Multibeam bathymetry image of the seafloor off Pillar Point showing the rock outcrops on the seafloor that give rise to the huge waves at Mavericks (in the boxed area). The rapid shallowing of the seafloor and the wedge-shaped patterns of the rocks concentrates wave energy under the right conditions.
COURTESY OF THE US GEOLOGICAL SURVEY.

Just over 16 years later, on March 16, 2011, Sion Milosky, another accomplished big-wave surfer from Hawaii, became Maverick's second victim. Sion suffered a two-wave hold-down at about 6:30 in the evening and apparently drowned. His body was found floating near the entrance of the Pillar Point harbor entrance about 20 minutes after the incident. While some big-wave surfers practice holding their breath underwater to prepare themselves for the inevitable wipeout and hold-down, the conditions beneath a literal mountain of water aren't quite the same as being in calm water, where you know which way is up. Sadly, Jay Moriarity, a young surfer who is the subject of the popular movie *Chasing Mavericks*, died while holding his breath underwater preparing for surfing large waves. As one of the youngest guys to surf Mavericks, he took one of the roughest wipeouts ever recorded.

Just 2 months before Sion's tragic death, Laguna Beach surfer Jacob Trette nearly drowned while surfing Mavericks after a bad wipeout. Jacob had been surfing since he was 4 years old. He and several other surfers were caught inside a wave and were frantically paddling to get over the crest of the wave before it broke. He didn't make it and went backward over the falls. He later recalled hitting the bottom feet first and pushing off. But there was another big wave and then three more, which knocked him out. Jacob essentially drowned that day but was picked up and rescued by photographer Russell Ord, who was on a jet ski, and taken to the beach, where they started CPR. The first responders continued CPR for about 13 minutes, until he began breathing again. He was transported to Stanford Medical Center in critical condition and put into an induced coma in cold water for 2 days to minimize brain damage. Fortunately, Jacob was able to make a full recovery. During a subsequent interview, he said he wanted to go back out at Mavericks but wanted to wear a life vest and make sure there were jet skis around.

Banzai Pipeline, on the north shore of Oahu, has often been called the deadliest surfing spot on the planet (see figure 3.6). The *Encyclopedia of Surfing* reports that a surfer dies here on average every other year. Eleven surfers have died there over the years, and hundreds of serious injuries have been recorded. Thirty surfers were injured at Pipeline on a single bad day in December 1998. This is not a place for the beginner or the inexperienced surfer, as tempting as it may appear.

The conditions that make this break potentially deadly are the same ones that make it exciting for the most experienced surfers and why it is the location for one of the profession's most prestigious yearly contests. Waves jack up quickly over a submerged reef just 200 feet from the beach. But Pipeline can be a wicked wave. Decisions have to be made in a few seconds about which wave to take and which line to follow, and any mistake or failure in split-second judgment can lead to serious injury or worse.

Waves at Pipeline don't have to be large to be dangerous and deadly, even to the most experienced surfers. Malik Joyeux was known for surfing huge barrels at his home break of Teahupo'o, and in 2003, he was given the Monster Energy Tube of the Year for what is considered one

Figure 3.6.   Wave breaking in shallow water over a reef at Banzai Pipeline, Oahu.
COURTESY OF FOSTER AND SONS, CC BY-SA 4.0 VIA WIKIMEDIA COMMONS.

of the biggest waves ever ridden there. An all-around waterman and one of Tahiti's most popular and accomplished surfers, he was known as an ambassador of Tahitian surfing. On December 2, 2005, Malik took off late on an 8-foot wave at Pipeline. He barely made the drop down the face of the wave and then tried to pull up under the lip but wasn't able to make it. The lip landed directly on Malik and drove him to the bottom. He was wearing a leash, but the board was broken and spit out by the breaking wave. Two larger waves followed, and after the second one, surfers and others on the beach started looking for him. About 15 minutes passed before one of the searchers found Malik's lifeless body about 100 yards up the beach. Despite CPR and a defibrillator, it was too late.

It's dangerous at Pipeline not only for those in the water but, because of the steep beach and strong backwash and currents, it also can be potentially fatal to those watching from the beach. The late Ricky Grigg, one of the first to surf Pipeline in 1961 and long a professor of oceanography at the University of Hawaii, recalls a large wave washing way up the shoreline on March 23, 1973, and pulling four women off the beach.

Several guys on the beach, including Grigg, jumped into the water to try to save them, but all four women died.

Cortes Bank rises a mile from the seafloor to within a few feet of the sea surface as part of an undersea mountain, 111 miles due west of San Diego. It was named by the captain of the steamship *Cortes* in 1853, who noticed waves breaking far out to sea over this submarine feature. The shallow bank was named after his ship and stuck. It seems like an unlikely place to go surfing, but from the observations of passing ships over the years, it was recognized that under the right conditions, in water more than 1,000 feet deep, truly mammoth waves would break at Cortes Bank.

It was more than a century later, in 1962, when Harrison Ealy, a surfer and a sailor from Laguna Beach, stopped at Cortes Bank on a sailing trip back from Hawaii. He got out his board, paddled over to a modest-sized wave, and became the first person to ever surf this spot in what appears to be the middle of the ocean. In the subsequent 58 years, the word about mountainous waves gradually slipped out, and Cortes Bank slowly became a magnet for a small group of hard-core big-wave surfers—including Peter Mel, Ken Collins, and Brad Gerlach—who were willing to endure the long boat trip from San Diego. Cortes Bank entered the legendary status of a handful of places around the planet where monster waves break under the right conditions. Jumping off a small boat with a 9- or 10-foot surfboard in what seems like the middle of the ocean to surf a wave that might be 50 to 75 feet high gets a lot of adrenaline flowing very quickly. It's a very different experience than being able to see the comfort of the shoreline a few hundred yards away.

December 21, 2012, was one of those days when the bank was breaking. Greg Long and three other big-wave surfers, Shane Dorian, Grant "Twiggy" Baker, and Ian Walsh, arrived on a 110-foot boat after the long 111-mile trip from San Diego. They were ready to have a go at this open ocean wave and had a rescue team of six jet ski operators they had brought along for safety, one for each surfer and two backups. Late in the afternoon, Greg dropped in too deep in the second of a five-wave set and made it to the bottom of the wave, when the whitewater from the broken wave overtook him and pushed him deep underwater. He tried to deploy his inflatable suit to get back to the surface quicker, but it failed to open. While he had trained himself for long hold-downs, because of the size of the wave, this one was particularly long and brutal.

Not sure when the next wave in the set was coming, he decided to swim for the surface. But a few feet from air, the next wave hit him with its full impact, forcing any remaining air from his tired lungs and pushing him back down into deep water. Greg was in a state of shock, with his lungs screaming for air; he tried to remain calm but needed to get to the surface soon. When the third wave hit, he realized he couldn't swim against it, so he tried to climb hand over hand up his leash until he reached his board, which was still 10 feet beneath the surface. Greg blacked out at this point, and the fourth wave pushed his now-unconscious body well inside the lineup, still attached to his board.

Through some heroic efforts, the jet ski support group was able to locate his body, face down in the water, and get him back to the boat. Still unconscious and in shock and after a bout of coughing up foamy blood, he was administered oxygen and checked for injuries. The Coast Guard was called, and a rescue helicopter was dispatched to Cortes Bank. Five hours later, in very large swells and in the dark, Greg Long was airlifted in a basket from the boat and taken back to a hospital in San Diego for a battery of tests. He was released to go home the next morning with no lasting physical injuries (see figure 3.7).

This near-death big-wave incident had a major emotional effect on Greg, however, which is recounted in his own words in a story in the October 1, 2014, issue of *Surfer* magazine. This experience led him to undergo a long period of introspection about what mattered in his life and what didn't. Greg was very fortunate, and through his own physical training and the skill of his rescue crew, he survived and had the opportunity both to surf big waves again and to obtain a clearer idea about his own life and its meaning.

There is clearly something in the blood of big-wave surfers that draws them to these immense walls of water—dangerous masses where things can go wrong fast, presenting huge personal challenges like Greg Long faced, as well as challenges for their partners on jet skis trying to find and rescue them after a wipeout. There is no question that there are

Figure 3.7.   Big-wave surfers Jeff Rowley (left) and Greg Long (right). Greg Long
nearly died surfing Cortes Bank.

enormous risks in taking off on a wave 50 to 75 feet high, in fact on any
large wave. While I spent a fair number of years surfing, when waves get
6 to 8 feet, I'm not out there. After wiping out on a modest 5-foot wave
and thinking I was going to die, I realized I value my life more than big-
wave adventures.

Like Hawaii and California, surfing is an iconic recreational activity
in Australia and is enjoyed by more than 2.5 million Australians, about
14 percent of the entire nation's population. Like many sports, surfing

can be amazingly thrilling and rewarding but also has the potential to be inherently dangerous. There's a lot of stuff than can go wrong in the coastal ocean, whether large waves or small, whether warm water or cold, and whether you are experienced or inexperienced. In 2011, a survey was carried out down under to get some sense of how accident prone Australian surfers actually are. What sorts of injuries and accidents are common, and what are the greatest risks these wave riders are exposed to? A website was set up and open for 12 months. Of the 772 active surfers spending on average 9 to 11 hours in the water per week who accessed the site, 685 of them (88.7 percent, a really high percentage for any survey) responded to the majority of the questions. Almost 40 percent indicated that they had sustained an injury in the past 12 months that was severe enough to keep them out of the water, at least for a while. Of these injuries, the most common listed involved knees (15.9 percent); ankles and feet (14.9 percent); torso (13.9 percent); shoulders (13.1 percent); head (12.8 percent); hips, groin, and legs (9.0 percent); neck and spine (7.9 percent); and arms and hands (6.9 percent). Nearly 20 percent of these (1 in 5) involved a trip to the hospital, but only 4.1 percent required a hospital stay.

These numbers might be surprising to active surfers. In contrast to contact sports (e.g., football, rugby, hockey), where players inflict as much damage as possible on opponents without getting penalized, in surfing there isn't usually anyone trying to injure you, and you have that nice, fluid seawater to fall into. But these statistics from Australia indicate that the probability of injury is fairly high and that nice, fluid water doesn't seem to matter a whole lot when you wipe out on a large wave.

Body surfers have their own spots to test their mettle. Perhaps the best known of these is the Wedge, at the end of the Balboa Peninsula at southern California's Newport Beach. Under the right conditions, generally a south swell, the incoming wave will reflect off the west jetty of Newport Harbor and reinforce or constructively interfere with the next incoming wave. This can produce a wedge-shaped wave up to a reported 20 to 30 feet in height but one that generally breaks in very shallow water. It's a shore break and not a place for beginners or the inexperienced, although that doesn't necessarily stop them from venturing out.

From daylight until 10:00 a.m., surfboards, boogie boards, and body boards are permitted at the Wedge, but then the blackball flag goes up, and only body surfers are allowed in the water. At least three body surfers have died from injuries at the Wedge, and many others have suffered broken necks and backs and partial paralysis, usually from the impact with the shallow seafloor beneath the breaking waves (see figures 3.8 and 3.9). The dangers are well known, but like many other sports where danger is involved, there is a magnetic attraction that pulls mostly boys and young

Figure 3.8.   Very large waves can form at the Wedge in Newport Beach as waves reflect off the jetty at the Newport Harbor entrance.
COURTESY OF CRAIG BERRY, CC BY 2.0 VIA FLICKR.

Figure 3.9. There have been more serious body-surfing injuries at the Wedge than at any other beach in southern California.
COURTESY OF SKIENGINEER, CC BY-SA 4.0 VIA WIKIMEDIA COMMONS.

men, as well as a few older guys, into this wedge-shaped wave for a few thrilling seconds but at a significant risk. The message here from these few accounts is that both board and body surfing are exciting and challenging, and for the great majority of those who enjoy these watersports, it is quite safe. Under certain conditions and in some individual locations, though, there can be significant risks that you need to be aware of, taking into account your own skill and limitations.

SCUBA DIVING

With the development of scuba (self-contained underwater breathing apparatus) nearly 80 years ago by Jacques Cousteau and Émile Gagnan, the natural curiosity of people for what lies beneath the sea surface can now be pursued relatively inexpensively (see figure 3.10). Training and certification opportunities expanded rapidly, and there are now about 6 million divers scattered around the planet, with about half of those active scuba divers in the United States. California, Florida, Texas, New

Figure 3.10.   Jacques Cousteau with early scuba gear.
FROM THE FILM SILENT WORLD, 1956; COURTESY OF THE EVERETT COLLECTION.

York, and the Virginia/Maryland/DC region, in that order, have the highest number of open-water-certified divers, making up 43 percent of the nation's total. Their average age is 35, and 71 percent are male. This is a sport that in general attracts well-educated people, with about two-thirds of these divers having completed college or graduate school and 62 percent holding managerial, technical, or professional jobs. Scuba diving contributes more than $2 billion annually to the global economy. It is a very big business.

While the great majority of dives are done recreationally, there are also professional divers involved in scientific, military, commercial, and public-safety roles. There are a number of both commercial and academic training programs for divers that provide different levels of certification and include learning the basic skills, the equipment and its limitations, general hazards to be keenly aware of when you are underwater, and self-help and assisting other divers with problems underwater. A minimum level of fitness and health is required by most training organizations.

Certainly, good visibility is important for any successful dive, and it tends to be those clear tropical waters, like in the Bahamas and the Caribbean, Hawaii, the South Pacific, the Great Barrier Reef, and the Red Sea, that attract the most numbers of divers, not only because of the clear water but also because of the astounding diversity of colorful tropical marine life (see figure 3.11). In cooler waters, along the California coast, for example, it is often the kelp forests that many divers explore. But seeking out more adventures, shipwrecks, and underwater caves in places like the Yucatan have attracted a new type of adventure diver.

Once you leave the surface, you enter an entirely new and generally silent world, one that grows darker as you go deeper and also one where the deeper you go and the longer you stay down, the more safety precautions and monitoring become necessary in order to return to the surface free of physiological problems.

Technical diving is scuba diving where the diver is stretching the normally accepted recreational diving limits. This may expose the diver to hazards beyond those typically associated with recreational diving and therefore to greater risk of significant injury and even death. In a word, the danger factor is amplified substantially. These increased risks can, however, be minimized by a combination of appropriate skills, experience, and knowledge and by using the right combination of equipment and safety procedures. Any dive where it is either not physically possible or physiologically acceptable to make a direct and uninterrupted vertical

Figure 3.11.   It is tropical underwater scenes like this that make scuba diving so attractive.
COURTESY OF CRAIG D. CC BY-SA 2.0, VIA FLICKR.

ascent to the surface is generally considered a technical dive. New equipment and various mixtures of gases that enable deeper, longer, and safer dives have been developed in recent years, but these still require significant training, experience, and care.

The underwater world can be fascinating and beautiful but also is unfamiliar and hazardous. Careful attention to detail and procedure and that the diver accepts responsibility for their own safety and survival are key. You cannot be too cautious in this sport. Most of the standard scuba-diving procedures are relatively straightforward and simple and become second nature to experienced divers. But these take some time and practice to learn and then systematically follow, just like many other activities. Danger can arise quickly when a beginner in any endeavor (e.g., driving a car or riding a motorcycle) is not yet familiar with the procedures and hazards and makes a single fatal mistake.

Diving fatalities (16.4 per 100,000 divers annually) are essentially identical to motor vehicle accidents (16 per 100,000 drivers) and jogging (13 deaths per 100,000 joggers per year). The risks of a fatal accident in normal recreational, scientific, or commercial diving are generally quite small. While using scuba, most deaths are associated with poor breathing-gas management, poor buoyancy control, misuse of equipment, entrapment, rough water conditions, and preexisting medical conditions. Some of these fatalities are inevitable and are a result of unanticipated situations that escalate out of control. The majority of diving deaths, however, can be attributed to human error by the victim. The cause is rarely equipment failure.

Based on death certificates, more than 80 percent of these deaths are ultimately attributed to drowning, although a number of other factors have usually conspired to incapacitate the diver in a series of events, which culminates in drowning. While there have not been statistical analyses, the contributing factors to these human errors usually include inexperience; infrequent diving; inadequate supervision; insufficient predive briefings; separation from the diver's buddy; and dive conditions beyond the diver's training, experience, or physical capacity. There are a finite number of things that can go wrong for a diver with a limited amount of experience 100 feet underwater, so a decision may have to be made relatively quickly in order to survive, and panic is not a good option.

FREE DIVING

Free diving, or diving without any breathing aids, is one of the earliest underwater activities to come into existence and has been practiced for centuries. Whether descending for seafood, sponges, coral, or pearls, this activity has been around for a long time. In Japan, Ama divers began to dive for pearls about 2,000 years ago. For thousands of years, most saltwater pearls were collected by divers working in the Indian Ocean in areas like the Persian Gulf and the Red Sea. Pearl divers near the Philippines also gathered pearls, especially in the Sulu Archipelago.

Over the years, a small group of men and women have challenged themselves to descend progressively deeper without any external air supply, simply by holding their breath as long as possible. Like so many sports, there are reputations to be earned and world records to be had, so there is an ongoing competition with these extreme divers. The average adult can hold their breath for about 30 seconds. With a little practice, some people can hold their breath for a minute or perhaps two (although this isn't something that I recommend you experiment with), but this is a piece of cake for these free divers. Most of the record-setting dives to depths of 300 to 400 feet require that divers hold their breath for 3 or 4 minutes or longer.

Perhaps not surprisingly, like many competitive sports, there are different categories of free-diving world records. These divers consider the purest form of free diving to be constant-weight free diving, where divers descend and ascend under their own power, although there are different categories depending on whether you use fins and whether you are a man or a woman. For men with fins (and these are very large fins), the record as of 2016 is 422 feet (120 meters), and for a woman, it is 334 feet (102 meters; see figure 3.12). Without fins, the depth record for a man is 334 feet, and for a woman, it is 235 feet. In my vast free-diving career, I think I've reached a depth of perhaps 20 feet at best, so to me, these are truly impressive accomplishments—but dangerous.

Another category of deep diving, which has extended the maximum depth, is variable-weight free diving, which allows the diver to use a weight to pull them down as deep as possible to extend their breath holding. They still, however, need to have enough oxygen left in their lungs to swim back to the surface using fins and pulling on a rope. For a man, the record is 477 feet (146 meters), and for a woman, it is 425 feet (130 meters), held by Nanja Den Broek, who holds 20 free-diving records.

The deepest dives fall under the no-limits free-diving category, where the diver can both use a weight to pull them down and a buoyancy-control device to assist them in returning to the surface. Tanya Streeter is the world champion female free diver and has gone as deep as 523 feet (160 meters). Herbert Nitsch set a new no-limits record in 2007 and descended to an astounding 702 feet (214 meters), earning the title "The Deepest Man on Earth," which is an honor I was previously unaware of (see figure 3.13). Herbert exceeded this depth 5 years later with a dive

Figure 3.12.   Meghan Grier free diving with fins.

Figure 3.13.   Herbert Nitsch earned the title of "The Deepest Man on Earth."

to 831 feet (253 meters) in the waters off Santorini, Greece. Taking advantage of the no-limits or no-holds-barred category, Nitsch used an innovative torpedo-type sled design with very high descent and ascent speed. He temporarily fell asleep due to nitrogen narcosis during the final part of the ascent and then woke up just prior to reaching the surface. Although he underwent post-dive decompression and was breathing medical oxygen, his condition became critical and required an emergency airlift to a decompression chamber in Athens.

He subsequently experienced multiple brain strokes and needed home care and use of a wheelchair. Through extensive rehabilitation, he did partially recover, although he still has balance and coordination problems, except when he is in the water. This seems like a high price to pay for "The Deepest Man on Earth" award. Herbert Nitsch is the only free diver to have gone beyond 800 feet. Just four others have dived beyond 560 feet, and two others have died trying. This is potentially a very dangerous sport with huge costs for pushing too hard.

Natalia Molchanva is considered by many to be the greatest free diver in history, until she disappeared off the coast of Spain during a recreational dive on a calm, sunny August morning in 2015. She had set a record for holding her breath in a pool for 9 minutes 2 years earlier. While a competitive swimmer in her youth in the Soviet Union, she took a 20-year break to raise a family, and then at age 40, after reading a magazine article about free diving, she decided to give it a try. In less than 10 years, she became the most respected free diver in the world.

Through what she called "attention deconcentration," she was able to turn inward, tune out distractions, and achieve a unique state allowing her to be completely in tune with her body. She worked up to the point where she could swim 595 feet underwater with one breath and no fins, the length of two football fields. She was the first woman to dive to 100 meters (327 feet) with weights. When she disappeared on that sunny August day in 2015, she was on a dive with friends at a depth that was insignificant to her, at just 115 feet. There was no swell, no wind, just the blue waters off the coast of Ibiza, Spain. She never surfaced, and while rescue divers, a robot submersible, and the Coast Guard all searched, she was never seen again. Again, the ultimate price to pay for becoming the most respected free diver in the world.

Thirteen years earlier, in October 2002, 28-year-old Audrey Mestre, a champion free diver, took a single breath and dove to 561 feet in an attempt to break a world record. Sadly, the young French woman did not make it back up alive. She and her husband Francisco "Pipin" Ferreras were the most famous free-diving couple on the planet. Audrey was trying on that October day to break the record that her husband had set 2 years earlier. While she reached the record depth, she blacked out at 300 feet on her return, and despite being rescued and brought to the surface by a safety diver, it was too late. While the dive was planned to take 3 minutes, she had been underwater without oxygen for 9 minutes.

There are about 5,000 free divers around the world, and an estimated 100 die each year—not good odds. Divers describe a sense of euphoria being so far down and compare the experience to being in outer space. It puts the body through some huge physiological changes and can be very liberating. But you need to stay completely aware of your body and where you are and remain entirely in the moment—easier said than done. In contrast to many other recreational activities or sports where probabilities of a fatal accident are very, very low, free diving falls into a completely different category.

CHAPTER FOUR

Dangerous Sea Creatures

On September 4, 2006, Steve Irwin, popular and much-loved television star of the *Crocodile Hunter*, environmentalist, conservationist, and wildlife expert, died after being stabbed in the chest by a stingray while filming on Australia's Great Barrier Reef. Irwin was part of a documentary series on the ocean's deadliest, and during a break in shooting he was snorkeling in shallow water when he approached a short-tail stingray from behind. From a person who observed the attack, the stingray was propped on its front and started stabbing wildly with its tail—hundreds of quick strikes. The barb pierced Irwin's heart, causing him to bleed to death. Despite his lifelong fascination of and filming with wild creatures, particularly dangerous ones, this encounter had an unexpected and tragic outcome.

The ocean contains approximately 228,000 individually named species, give or take a few, but there's a consensus that there are probably far more that haven't yet been identified, most in the microscopic category. This number includes everything from tiny microbes to the largest animal on the planet, the gigantic blue whale—at nearly 100 feet long and weighing 200 tons—larger than any dinosaur that ever roamed the Earth. Of this roughly quarter-million different species, there are just 10 or so that are truly dangerous, like able-to-kill-you dangerous: just 0.00004 percent of all ocean organisms.

With a few exceptions, most dangerous ocean animals are found in the tropical and subtropical Pacific and Indian Oceans, far from where most of us enjoy the ocean. As the global climate and ocean water continue to warm, many tropical and subtropical organisms are gradually expanding their ranges and migrating farther north and south into what were formerly cooler waters.

These potentially dangerous creatures fall into two major categories, depending on the threat they pose: those that are large, with big teeth, and can bite you or could completely swallow you if given the chance, and those that are considerably smaller, without huge teeth but use stinging or venom to stun or capture their prey. The former definitely looks dangerous and should be avoided. While humans aren't natural prey for the latter, there is a potential for serious impacts if stung.

What are these creatures, and what do we know about them? How concerned should we be? The following pages describe the top 10 dangerous ocean animals found on most lists.

LARGE ANIMALS THAT POSE A SERIOUS THREAT FROM A BITE

There are only 2 of the top 10 that use teeth when they attack, primarily to catch and then consume their prey. And both have large enough teeth to do a lot of damage with a single bite, which should be avoided at all costs.

Great White Shark

Entire volumes have been written and full-length movies made about great white sharks. They just grab our attention more so than probably any other animal living in the ocean because of their size, their row upon row of very sharp teeth, and the widely publicized stories and images of attacks or close encounters with unsuspecting people in the water.

Sharks are survivors and have been on the planet for more than 400 million years. If we were to compress the entire 4.5 billion years of Earth history into an epic 3-hour movie, our species, *Homo sapiens*, would have been around for the past one-half second, or only about 200,000 years. In contrast, sharks, which have often been called "living fossils," would have been in the 3-hour movie for the last 17 minutes, or for at least 420 million years. Sharks appeared on the evolutionary scene well before dinosaurs, and while the dinosaurs disappeared about 65 million years ago, sharks have survived and continued to flourish, although human predation on sharks in recent years has taken a large toll.

The great white shark of today (*Carcharodon cacharias*) can be quite large, with the biggest caught being 21 feet long and weighing 3.6 tons, or about the weight of the biggest Ford or Dodge mega-pickup truck. One of the challenges facing paleontologists studying fossils of ancient sharks, however, is that there isn't a whole lot of stuff that is usually left behind after a shark dies. Have you ever seen a shark skeleton on display, with all the vertebrae and ribs? Probably not, because instead of bones, sharks have a cartilaginous skeleton, like some fish, and this soft stuff decomposes too quickly for fossilization to occur.

Typically, it's the hard teeth of these prehistoric sharks that are preserved. One shark in particular, the megalodon (from the Greek words for big or mighty tooth), was so massive that it could have eaten a great white shark of today for breakfast (see figure 4.1). The teeth from these

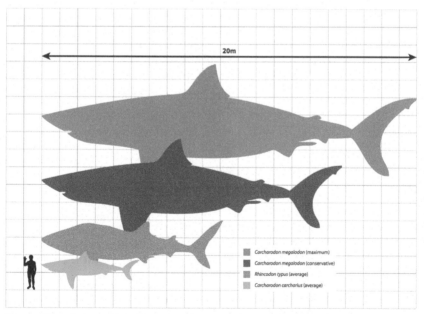

Figure 4.1.   Comparative sizes of ancient and modern sharks with the size of an average person.
COURTESY OF SCARLET23, CC BY-SA 3.0 VIA WIKIMEDIA COMMONS.

creatures are alarmingly huge, up to 7 inches long. Think of your hand with all your fingers outstretched—and that's just one tooth! Based on relationships between the size of teeth and body length and mass for modern sharks, the best estimates are that megalodon was 50 to 70 feet long and weighed somewhere in the range of 60 to 100 tons. This is like a very large city transit bus with fins and 7-inch teeth. Fortunately for us and for everything else living in the sea today, the megalodon died out about 2.5 million years ago. No one is quite sure why, as information from 2.5 million years ago is scarce, although it may have been a combination of changing water temperatures and food availability. An animal weighing at least 60 tons needs to consume a lot of food every day.

Of the roughly 350 species of sharks found in the oceans today, only 35 of those have been known to attack humans, and only 4 are recognized as significant threats. Great white sharks seem to gather the most attention because they are more common in US and Australian waters and because they have been responsible for more attacks on humans than any other type of shark. They live in almost all coastal and offshore waters around the planet that have water temperatures between about 54°F and 75°F, with greater concentrations in the coastal waters of the United States (the southeast and California), South Africa, Japan, Oceania, Chile, and the Mediterranean. An attack from any of the four most dangerous sharks (great white shark, striped tiger shark, bull shark, and blacktip shark) has the potential to be deadly, although fatalities from shark attacks are surprisingly rare relative to almost any other risks in our daily lives.

Between 2014 and 2018, an average of 82 confirmed and unprovoked shark attacks have taken place, with just four fatalities globally each year. Without question, the number of human-shark interactions strongly correlates with the time that people spend in the water, with both the number of people in the water and ocean-related activities increasing. For 2019, the most recent year of complete records, the United States led the world with 41 unprovoked attacks, or almost two-thirds of the world's total, followed by Australia with eleven. Within US waters, Florida is at the top of the list for the greatest number of attacks, with 21, or half of the total, followed by Hawaii with nine, and California and North Carolina with three each. What were those people doing when attacked? Surfers and those involved with board sports accounted for more than half of the incidents, with those swimming or wading accounting for another 25 percent. The others were snorkeling, body surfing, or scuba diving, all considered unprovoked attacks. In contrast, provoked attacks are encounters where the person was foolishly prodding or provoking a shark. These are the sorts of people who often win Darwin Awards for practicing unwise behaviors that tend to take them out of the gene pool.

In California, since 1900, there have been only 180 confirmed unprovoked attacks or encounters with great white sharks. This is an average of only 1.5 per year, which, considering the millions of beachgoers, swimmers, surfers, divers, and others in nearshore waters, is a remarkably low number. In the last 40 years, there have been 10 fatalities along the state's coast, all believed to be from great white sharks. This translates to 1 fatality every 4 years on average. For comparison, during just 4 weeks of the winter of 2020–2021, 10 people died along California's coast after being swept off rocks or caught by large waves along the shoreline.

The total number of unprovoked shark attacks worldwide is still very low, considering the vast number of people using coastal waters for various recreational activities, and fatality rates have been declining for decades due to progress in public education and awareness, warning systems, beach safety, and first aid. Fishing for sharks has greatly reduced their numbers, so there are fewer of them in the water. In most coastal states, beaches are posted with signs for a few days after a shark attack or sighting. In Australia, some popular beaches have been protected with nets for years to keep sharks away. Overall, however, with the millions of beachgoers and thousands of miles of shoreline, keeping sharks away from beaches is essentially an impossible task.

The odds of being attacked by a shark during a beach visit is about 1 in 11.5 million. The probability of being killed by a shark is 1 in 264 million. All this is not to say that great white sharks don't pose any danger to humans in the water, but relative to virtually anything else you can imagine, the risk of a fatal shark attack is extremely low.

Saltwater Crocodile

No listing of ocean predators is complete without some huge, scary reptile with a mouthful of large teeth. The saltwater crocodile, or salties, as they are often called, are generally known as the most dangerous animal of Australia. These large reptiles inhabit river deltas and brackish-water mangrove swamps extending in a broad arc from the east coast of India, through Sri Lanka, Bangladesh, Myanmar, Thailand, Malaysia, Cambodia, Vietnam, Indonesia, the Philippines, Palau, the Solomon Islands, Vanuatu, and south, all the way to Australia's north coast. If you trace that on a map, you can quickly see that it's quite a large area of tropical ocean.

These reptiles exhibit among the greatest sexual dimorphism (difference in size of the two sexes) of any animal. The males can be truly massive, up to 20 feet in length and weighing more than a ton (see figure 4.2). In contrast, adult females usually reach only about half this size and

Figure 4.2.   A large male Australian saltwater crocodile.
COURTESY OF MOLLY EBERSOLD, ST. AUGUSTINE ALLIGATOR FARM, PUBLIC DOMAIN VIA WIKIMEDIA COMMONS.

weigh perhaps only 450 pounds. With their size, though, comes lethal power; these big crocs have the most powerful known bite in the animal world, with a jaw having about 10 times more strength than that of a great white shark. Salties live both on land and in saltwater. They can move very quickly in the water, 15 to 18 miles per hour in short bursts, about 3 times faster than the fastest human swimmer, so you will not escape one of these beasts by swimming away from them.

They are deceptively fast on land, and while they might not be as fast as some horror stories report, they can attack quicker than most humans can react. Of all the crocodilian species, the saltwater and Nile crocodiles have the strongest tendency to treat humans as prey. The saltwater crocodile has a long recorded history of attacking humans who unknowingly or naïvely trespass into their territory.

Because of its power, intimidating size, and speed, survival of a direct predatory attack is unlikely if the animal is able to make contact with any part of your body. With their very large mouths, a male saltwater crocodile can essentially swallow you whole, which is a rather depressing thought. In contrast to the American policy of encouraging a certain degree of habitat coexistence with alligators, the only recommended policy for dealing with saltwater crocodiles is to completely avoid their habitat, as they are extremely aggressive when encroached on or approached.

Exact data on attacks on humans are limited outside Australia, where 1 to 3 fatal attacks are commonly reported each year. There were 106 deaths from crocodile attacks down under in the 42-year period between 1971 and 2013. This relatively low number is probably in part due to efforts by wildlife officials to post crocodile warning signs at numerous at-risk rivers, lakes, and beaches. Many attacks outside Australia, throughout Southeast Asia, are believed to go unreported due to the very rural nature of these areas and, generally, low populations. One study reported that up to 20 to 30 attacks occur each year. Some attacks on humans appear to be more territorial rather than predatory, with mature crocodiles usually attacking anything that enters their area, including small boats.

These large reptiles are indiscriminate or opportunistic feeders, however, and across their range, they have been known to attack and eat water birds; crabs and fish; amphibians; small to medium-sized mammals (including deer, monkeys, rabbits, and rodents); and domestic livestock, such as goats, pigs, chickens, sheep, and even cattle and horses—and then humans when they are on the menu. All things considered, it's best to just avoid them and give these bad boys a very wide berth.

ANIMALS WITH THE CAPABILITY OF STINGING AND INJECTING VENOM
Box Jellyfish

One of the most dangerous sea creatures lurking around out there doesn't have rows of razor-sharp teeth (or any visible mouth at all), but it has caused more human deaths in Australia than snakes, sharks, and saltwater crocodiles combined. These creatures are transparent and pale blue in color, which makes them almost invisible in the water. It took years before anyone even realized what was causing such agonizing pain for unsuspecting swimmers and divers. Unlike other jellyfish that float with the currents, these cnidarians can propel themselves up to about 5 to 6 feet per second, not exactly the speed of a tuna or swordfish, but fast enough to catch their prey. So rather than waiting for some morsel to come to them, box jellyfish can actually hunt small fish, shrimp, and crabs.

These little jellies only grow to about 12 inches in diameter, although their tentacles can reach almost 10 feet in length, and there are usually about 15 tentacles on each corner of their box-shaped bodies (see figure 4.3). Each of these long appendages has about 500,000 cnidocytes (yep, 500,000), or explosive cells—each with nematocysts (harpoon-shaped stinging mechanisms) that can inject venom into a victim. One box jellyfish, also known as a sea wasp, contains enough venom theoretically to kill up to 60 adult humans. What makes them even more dangerous is their venom's speed of acting: the sting from the tentacles of a box jellyfish can kill you in less than 3 to 5 minutes. To make matters worse, even if you aren't stung with a large dose of venom, the pain is so excruciating that it has been known to cause shock, which can lead to drowning.

Although the most dangerous species of this jellyfish are restricted mainly to the tropical Indo-Pacific region, some species can be found broadly in tropical and subtropical oceans, including in the Atlantic and

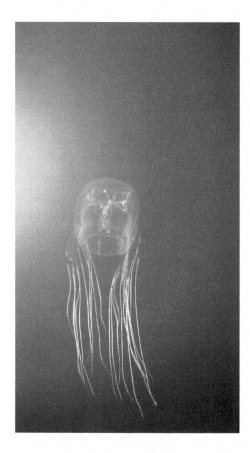

Figure 4.3.   Box jellyfish with tentacles.
COURTESY OF GUIDO GAUTSCH, CC BY-SA 2.0 VIA FLICKR.

eastern Pacific. Some species are found as far north as California, the Mediterranean, and Japan, and as far south as South Africa and New Zealand.

While the box jellyfish has been labeled the "world's most venomous creature," there are actually only a few species that have been shown to be involved in the death of humans, and some species pose no substantial threat at all; that's a little reassuring as long as you know which is which. One species that frequents Australian waters has caused at least 64 deaths since first reported more than a century ago. In the Malay Archipelago, however, lethal stings are far greater, with an estimated 20 to 40 fatalities annually, perhaps because of the limited access to medical treatment and availability of antivenom drugs.

Some popular Australian beaches are now protected with nets and also have containers with vinegar placed at strategic locations for immediate treatment. Washing with vinegar can deactivate undischarged nematocysts to prevent the release of additional venom. These stinging cells can still discharge venom even after the jellyfish is dead, a somewhat frightening feature—sort of postmortem revenge. Although there is a lot of folklore and publications on sting treatment, there is no scientific evidence that urine, ammonia, meat tenderizer (what would you be doing with meat tenderizer at the beach anyway?), lemon juice, freshwater, alcohol, papaya, or hydrogen peroxide will disable the nematocysts, and in fact, they may actually hasten venom release. It's best to just avoid these box jellies or keep some vinegar in your backpack just in case you are in their waters.

Stonefish

The stonefish is generally accepted as the most venomous fish in the world, and while mainly found in the ocean, some are known to live in rivers and have even survived on the beach for up to 24 hours. The name comes from their camouflage coloration, which looks virtually indistinguishable underwater from a rock on the seafloor (see figure 4.4). Like many other dangerous sea creatures, their habitat is the general Indo-Pacific region, and they are relatively common in Australian waters.

There's got to be something about the warm waters of the Indo-Pacific and Australia that serves as a magnet for these dangerous marine animals. It is also likely that as the oceans continue to warm, these potentially dangerous tropical or subtropical animals will gradually move into waters farther north and south that are presently too cool for them. This has been observed for some time with certain species. Humboldt squid, for example, common in warmer waters to the south of Mexico, are becoming frequent inhabitants in California coastal waters, where they were rarely seen historically.

Stonefish aren't usually more than about 12 inches long, but they are living proof that you don't have to be large in order to be a threat. Their venom can cause excruciating pain, temporary paralysis, and even heart failure for anyone with a weak or compromised heart. The reassuring fact

Figure 4.4.   A well-camouflaged stonefish.
COURTESY OF JULIE BEDFORD, NATIONAL OCEANIC AND ATMOSPHERIC ADMINISTRATION, CORAL
KINGDOM COLLECTION, VIA FLICKR.

for divers or snorkelers is that stonefish won't attack you. These camouflaged creatures use their venom only as a defensive mechanism and kill
their prey with quick attacks instead; they are reportedly able to attack
and swallow their prey in less than a second. Despite this attack speed,
they are generally very slow swimmers.

It's the 13 dorsal fins you have to be wary of, which are erect when
the fish is threatened and are sharp enough to pierce a shoe. Watching
your step in shallow water is the best precaution, which is challenging
due to their natural camouflage. Getting pierced by the dorsal fin will
produce agonizing pain, cause flesh around the wound to die, produce
swelling for months, and could result in amputation if not treated right
away. A large dose of venom without treatment, which involves antibi-
otics and antivenom, could even lead to death. In addition to antivenom,

hot water applied to the area of the sting has been found to denature the venom. Vinegar is also believed to lessen the pain.

In the 1-year period between July 1989 and June 1990, Australia reported 25 cases of the use of stonefish antivenom, with most of these in Queensland and the Northern Territory. In 2008, there were 14 calls to the Queensland Information System regarding stonefish poison. While there are a considerable number of stings recorded each year, there are no recorded deaths since Europeans arrived in Australia; this is believed to be due to the development of antivenom drugs in the late 1950s. So agonizing pain is likely if you are unfortunate enough to step on one of these camouflaged fish, but death is unlikely.

Interestingly, if properly prepared, stonefish are considered a delicacy in parts of Asia and are believed to be good for one's health. However, it is crucial to carefully remove the dorsal fins, the main source of the venom, prior to eating.

Blue-Ringed Octopus

The tiny and beautiful but deadly blue-ringed octopus may only be 5 to 8 inches in length but reportedly carries enough venom to kill more than 20 people within minutes (see figure 4.5). Yet, there apparently are records of only three people being killed by this creature: two in Australia and one in Singapore. These venomous little cephalopods are found in coral reefs and tide pools in the Indian and Pacific Oceans, from Japan to Australia. They are not creatures you want to mess with, and the good news is that they don't want to mess with you, either. They are relatively docile and are only dangerous to humans if provoked, stepped on, or handled because of their venom, a powerful neurotoxin known as tetrodotoxin.

They spend much of their time hiding in cracks or crevices while exhibiting typical octopus camouflage coloring and patterns with their chromatophore cells. When threatened, they can quickly change colors—in less than a second—and will become bright yellow with each of the 50 to 60 circular patches or rings flashing iridescent blue as a warning. The rings contain multilayer light reflectors known as iridophores, which are arranged to reflect blue-green light in a wide-viewing direction. In addition to changing colors, they can also change their shape.

Figure 4.5.   Blue-ringed octopus.

The blue-ringed octopus typically feeds on small crabs and shrimp but will also go after injured fish. It pounces on prey, grabbing it with its arms, and pulling it toward its mouth. It then uses its very hard, sharp beak to break through the exoskeleton of the crab or shrimp, releasing venom, which paralyzes the muscles of the victim required for movement, effectively killing its dinner.

Adding to the danger of this little 8-inch creature is that the bite itself is relatively painless, so you may not even know you've been injected until you start feeling the symptoms. Direct contact with the octopus is necessary to be envenomated (injected with venom), and when facing danger, the octopus's first reaction is to flee. If the threat persists, however, it will take a defensive stance and show its characteristic blue rings, which is your warning not to get any closer. If cornered or touched, there is a high risk of being bitten, and the tetrodotoxin can cause severe and often total body paralysis. While a victim may be fully aware of their surroundings, they will typically be unable to move, leaving them no way to signal for help or to indicate they are in distress. This effect is temporary, however, and will fade over a period of perhaps 24 hours as the toxin is metabolized and excreted by the body. Not surprisingly, children are generally at the greatest risk because of their small size.

There is no effective antidote to the venom, and the only remedy is to treat the symptoms until the venom dissipates. First-aid treatment is direct pressure on the bite and artificial respiration once the paralysis has disabled the victim's respiratory muscles, which typically occurs within minutes. Victims can be saved if artificial respiration is started and continued or until medical assistance arrives and gets the person into a hospital and onto a ventilator until the body removes the toxin. Slightly encouraging, those who survive the first 24 hours usually recover completely.

These little creatures only live for about 2 years. To make matters worse, a male blue-ringed octopus dies soon after mating. The female lays the eggs and incubates them under her arms for about 6 months. She doesn't feed during this entire time, and after the eggs hatch, she dies of starvation. Life is a little rough and short for a blue-ringed octopus.

Lionfish

On a trip to the Bahamas several years ago, my wife and I were snorkeling in warm, clear, and relatively shallow water. There weren't a lot of fish around, but I did see a beautiful fish not far away, which we both swam toward to get a closer look. We were within 8 to 10 feet of this creature when the realization hit me that we were looking at an actual lionfish. We slowly backed off, watched from a distance, and then swam away with an eye toward any others that might have been nearby.

Lionfish are part of the scorpion fish family. Although they are among the most beautiful fish in the oceans (see figure 4.6), it's probably best not to get too close. One of the two lionfish species, *Pterois volitans*, has been described as "one of the most aggressively invasive species on the planet," which sounds like the description of an animal we should carefully avoid. While a sting from a lionfish is not usually fatal, it can

Figure 4.6. A lionfish with spines extended.
COURTESY OF ALEXANDER VASENIN, CC BY-SA 3.0 VIA WIKIMEDIA COMMONS.

provide a very painful injection with some powerful venom. Their venomous spines won't kill you, but they contain a toxin so painful that it is described as making you wish you were dead. The diverse effects include extreme pain, nausea, vomiting, fever, breathing difficulties, convulsions, dizziness, numbness, headache, and heartburn—in short, extreme discomfort and pain. Death can occur in very young children, the elderly, those with weak immune systems, and those with allergic reactions to the venom. It may be encouraging to know that lionfish use their gruesome stings only defensively—they won't lie in ambush ready to inject you. If you are diving in the Caribbean or along the South Atlantic or Gulf coasts of the United States, it is recommended that you admire these beautiful, white-striped creatures from a distance.

Like many other deadly creatures, lionfish are native to the Indo-Pacific region and are usually found around the seaward edge of reefs, in lagoons, and to depths of about 150 feet. They prey aggressively on small fish and invertebrates but also are typically hostile and territorial toward other reef fish. Some researchers have also reported aggression toward scientists attempting to study them. While initially native to tropical and subtropical waters extending from southern Korea and Japan to the east coast of Australia, Indonesia, Micronesia, and French Polynesia, they are also found in the Indian Ocean all the way to the Red Sea.

In recent years, 2 of the 12 species of lionfish have established populations in the Caribbean and also along the Gulf and Atlantic coasts of the United States. The lionfish invasion is considered one of the most serious recent threats to Caribbean and Florida coral reef ecosystems. What is not completely clear is whether this expanding range is due to the continuing warming of the global oceans, thus extending the comfortable range of the lionfish to more northerly latitudes, or, like so many other marine organisms, a product of the transport of eggs and larvae in the ballast water of ships. About 95 percent of all our commerce moves by sea and many ships carry ballast water for stabilization when empty. When reaching the destination port, the ballast water from the port of origin is discharged and, along with it, any included eggs and larvae. These new, exotic, alien species may thrive in their new home and often lack natural predators, so they can reproduce and thrive and may cause major ecological disruption or instability by outcompeting or overwhelming the native populations.

It is thought that the damage from Hurricane Andrew in 1992, which destroyed an aquarium in southern Florida, may have been the source of the first invaders. Additionally (and this problem is not unique to the lionfish), home aquarists and collectors of exotic animals often find that their collection is too much trouble and then naïvely release the animals into the wild. Whatever the original source, adult lionfish are now found in nearshore waters extending from Cape Hatteras to Florida and along the Gulf Coast as far west as Texas, as well as in Bermuda, the Bahamas, the Cayman Islands, Aruba, Curaçao, Trinidad and Tobago, Haiti, Cuba, Mexico, Belize, Honduras, and Columbia, and as far south as Brazil.

These beautiful but dangerous fish have found fertile waters for invading, and population densities continue to increase. This fish has some temperature tolerances that may play a role in their survival, reproduction, and distribution range. They appear to have few predators that have enough venom resistance to survive an encounter.

Several different eradication strategies have been developed to reduce and control the population, including species-specific traps, organized and government-sponsored removal campaigns by divers, and a "lionfish as food" campaign. As has been learned from other foreign plants and animals, however, completely removing or eradicating invasive species in the ocean is a massive and labor-intensive challenge once the species has become established. Participants in the September 2021 Florida Keys Lionfish Derby and Festival speared 1,215 lionfish in 2 days. Four spearfishermen working together speared 564 of the invasive fish.

Flower Urchin

The flower urchin has made its way to the *Guinness Book of Records* as the world's "most dangerous sea urchin"—and for good reason. Like so many others in the top 10, they are common in the tropical Indo-Pacific region, extending from Okinawa, Japan, in the north to Tasmania, Australia, in the south and from the Red Sea in the west to the Cook Islands in the east. Their range is broad and includes coral reefs, seagrass beds, and rocky or sandy settings from shallow water to depths of about 300 feet.

Their generic name, *Toxopneustes*, literally means poison breath, and this urchin is in a league of its own when it comes to painful defensive mechanisms. As many have learned the hard way, stepping on a sea urchin can be very unpleasant because of their many spines. This urchin has a large number of distinct, flowerlike pedicellarie (hence the common name, flower urchin), usually yellowish-white to pinkish-white in color and on stalks, which rise above the urchin's short, blunt spines (see figure 4.7). Unlike other urchins that deliver venom through their spines, the flower urchin transmits their poison through their pedicellarie. These triangular-shaped appendages have claws in them, which can inject a toxic cocktail of chemicals.

Unlike other sea urchins, the stings of these creatures not only cause intense pain but can also lead to short-term paralysis, which may even

Figure 4.7.   A flower urchin with the pedicellariae extended.
COURTESY OF PHILIPPE BOURJON, CC BY-SA 3.0 VIA WIKIMEDIA COMMONS.

end in death if the victim is underwater. They possess claw-like structures that can break off the stalks, adhere to whatever they came into contact with and continue injecting venom for several hours. Reports of death are generally unconfirmed, but for those who are stung, responses include muscular paralysis, difficulty breathing, numbness, and disorientation, which can result in accidental drowning. Again, like the other dangerous creatures on this list, it's best to avoid these echinoderms. A common habit of the flower urchin—like other urchins—is to cover themselves with algae, dead coral fragments, shells, and other objects, making them blend into their surroundings and complicating human avoidance.

Stingray

Although the Crocodile Hunter, Steve Irwin, was killed by an Australian short-tailed or bull ray, one of the largest species of stingrays, your chances of being attacked by a stingray are very low. In fact, if Irwin wouldn't have died this way, stingrays may not even be on this list. Fatal stings are extremely rare, and his death in 2006 was only the second recorded in Australian waters since 1945.

While stingrays may appear dangerous (in part due to their name), these large and majestic creatures don't hunt for divers and swimmers, and a sting would generally only take place if you stepped on one. Stingrays are one of the more passive ocean creatures and hardly ever attack, but when incidents do take place, it's almost always thought to be a defense mechanism from a diver's or swimmer's accidental contact. Although they do have venom, most do not cause serious injury, but there are a few that can inject enough poison to be fatal. Contact with the stinger can cause local trauma, pain, swelling, and muscle cramps from the venom, painful but rarely life threatening. The barb may break off in the wound, which could require surgery for removal. Other than these few potential inconveniences, these animals generally are not creatures to be frightened of—cautious of but not frightened.

There are about 220 known stingray species scattered around the world's oceans, and they are gradually becoming more vulnerable to extinction from unregulated fishing. Forty-five species were listed in 2013 as vulnerable or endangered by the International Union for the Conservation of Nature (IUCN).

Related to sharks, rays are cartilaginous fish, with a skeleton of cartilage rather than bone. They are relatively common in coastal tropical or subtropical waters throughout the world's oceans, and there are several species that are only found in freshwater. Some stingrays can camouflage themselves by changing colors, depending on bottom conditions, and they also commonly bury themselves in the sand to hide from potential prey (see figure 4.8).

Rays vary widely in size, from the giant oceanic manta ray, which may weigh more than two tons and have a wingspan of more than 20 feet, to the longheaded eagle ray, which doesn't usually reach 20 pounds and is just 10 to 20 inches across. The giant oceanic manta ray is widely distributed in both tropical and temperate waters globally and has been seen as far north as southern California and New Jersey in the United States, as well as in Japan, the Azores, Peru, Uruguay, South Africa, and even New Zealand. These big guys may either travel alone or have been

Figure 4.8.   A large Southern stingray.
COURTESY OF THE NATIONAL OCEANIC AND ATMOSPHERIC ADMINISTRATION, CCMA BIOGEOGRA-
PHY TEAM, CORAL KINGDOM COLLECTION, VIA FLICKR.

seen in groups of up to 50 and have also been observed swimming with marine mammals.

About 25 percent of the diet of these large rays comes from filter feeding, like baleen whales, and they consume large volumes of plankton, including krill, shrimp, and pelagic crabs. The rest of their food is usually in deeper water and includes fish. Because they are so large and can swim fast, they have few natural predators: only a few species of large sharks, dolphins, and killer whales. Their primary threat is from fishing, and their population has been significantly decreased in recent years due to overfishing. Because large rays reach sexual maturity quite late, have a long gestation period, and only give birth to a single pup, they are at a far greater risk of population decline than other fish. Most smaller rays give birth to larger litters of live young, generally 5 to 13 in a litter.

Cone Snail

In contrast to most of the deadly animals in the ocean that actually look dangerous, like great white sharks or saltwater crocodiles, the cone snail is about as passive and helpless looking as you could imagine. There are more than 800 different species of these snails. Most are only a few inches long, but some are as long as 8 or 9 inches. In addition to the Indo-Pacific, some species live in the cool waters off southern California and Florida, in the Mediterranean Sea, and along the Cape Coast of South Africa. They can be found from the intertidal zone to deeper off-shore water living on sand or among rocks on reefs. Many of these snails are brightly colored, with intricate geometric markings or patterns (see figure 4.9). They are exactly the kind of shell we are all looking for when we go beachcombing in tropical waters. However, you could be taking a significant risk by picking up one of these shells if the snail is still alive.

Figure 4.9.   A cone snail with its characteristic intricate color patterns.
COURTESY OF HARRY ROSE, CC BY 2.0 VIA FLICKR.

Cone snails are nothing like the common snail that feasts on your lettuce, basil, and whatever else you planted in your garden, but rather they are carnivorous and predatory. They search for and devour small fish, worms, mollusks, and surprisingly even other cone snails. I guess we could call them cannibal snails. Like all snails, they move quite slowly, but they compensate for their lack of speed by having a venomous harpoon-like appendage that is hollow and barbed. When the snail senses prey close by, it extends a long, flexible tube—called a proboscis—toward it. This appendage contains venom that is fired with a muscular contraction. The venom is powerful enough to paralyze even a small fish almost instantly. The cone snail then retracts the appendage and draws the animal into its mouth, where it is digested, with any indigestible hard parts like teeth, spines, or scales regurgitated later.

With their beautifully colored and patterned shells, they are an attractive but risky target for shell collectors. If picked up, the snail just may fire its harpoon. The harpoon is even capable of penetrating a diver's gloves and wetsuits. For many species, their stings are comparable to those of a bee or wasp. The larger varieties, however, those that eat tropical fish, have a much more dangerous venom that can be fatal. One of these larger cone snails has been known locally as the cigarette snail because after being stung by one of these mollusks, the victim will have only enough time to smoke a cigarette before dying (an exaggeration).

Symptoms of a serious sting can include intense, localized pain and swelling, numbness, tingling, and vomiting. Somewhat bizarre, these symptoms can start immediately or may not occur for several days. In particularly severe cases, muscle paralysis, vision disruption, and respiratory failure can lead to death. Records indicate only 27 human deaths can confidently be blamed on cone snails. All in all, these are pretty low odds, but knowing what potential medical problems can ensue from a sting, it's best to avoid the temptation to pick up a beautiful and intricately patterned shell—that may have a potentially dangerous mollusk lurking within.

Sea Snake

Sea snakes, which are part of the cobra family of vipers, include about 47 different species that are most likely to be encountered in the tropical waters of the Pacific and Indian Oceans. The range of one species, however, extends from northern New Zealand to the Gulf of California, with isolated individuals occasionally found as far north as San Diego and Oxnard, California. This gives them a geographic range greater than any other reptile except for a few species of sea turtles. They prefer shallow water near land, around islands, and typically somewhat calmer waters and have been even found in estuaries and rivers.

Sea snakes have adapted well to an aquatic existence, with a paddlelike tail that improves their swimming ability (see figure 4.10). Their ventral scales are reduced in size, however, which makes them nearly helpless on land. While they can only crawl awkwardly on the beach or on land, they also can become aggressive in these settings, striking out at anything moving nearby. They breathe air, so they usually have part of their heads above water when swimming.

Snakes are believed to be the most abundant reptiles on the planet, and there have been frequent reports of swarms or schools of several hundred sea snakes swimming together. This would likely be a bit disconcerting if you happened to be in the water when one of these schools approaches. In the Gulf of Panama, drift lines more than a mile long containing hundreds of sea snakes are common. Why these massive aggregations occur isn't well understood, but one likely reason is that it has to do with reproduction; after all, being surrounded by tens of thousands of your own species makes it highly likely that you would find a compatible mate.

Sea snakes aren't aggressive reptiles and are most often considered mild tempered and reluctant to bite. Most species are venomous, however, and seem to use their venom mostly for defense, although there are species that use it to immobilize their prey. Even when bitten and injected with venom, most humans initially have very minor to nonexistent symptoms that may not even be noticed at the time. The venom is slow acting, however, and symptoms may not be apparent for 30 minutes or several hours after a bite and can include general aching, headache,

Figure 4.10.   A poisonous sea snake.

thirst, sweating, and vomiting. This can be followed later by a progressive paralysis, gradually affecting swallowing and respiration, which in very rare cases can be fatal. In fact, the death of a fisherman off Australia in 2018 was that country's first reported sea-snake fatality since a pearl diver was fatally bitten in 1935. This is good news for those Australians with ophidiophobia or ophiophobia, or a fear of snakes.

It's always helpful to know the dangers you might see or encounter when you go on a trip. There are potentially harmful sea creatures scattered around the oceans of the planet, and becoming aware of those animals that inhabit the waters you plan on swimming is a good idea. It is strongly recommended that you keep your distance from those big animals in the water with large teeth and those that can sting or inject you with venom.

The waters of the Indo-Pacific region, including Australia, are where these animals are most common. It seems that the warm, clear, tropical waters that attract us on our travels are the same environments that these creatures favor and inhabit. But these potentially threatening creatures are not limited to tropical waters, and at least half of the top 10 also inhabit or have migrated into more temperate waters: the Mediterranean, South Africa, the Gulf and South Atlantic coasts of the United States, and even the waters off southern California. With a few exceptions, however, most of these animals are not aggressive and will only bite or sting if touched, threatened, or agitated. Recognition and avoidance is always the best strategy. There are some other potentially dangerous or deadly beasts not on this list that are also lurking out there, and this chapter isn't intended to cover them all; the animals in this chapter are only those that are thought to be of greatest concern. The chances of being bitten or stung is actually very low for most of us and typically happens when someone intentionally or inadvertently threatens one of these creatures. This is not a common occurrence, however, and even when it happens, it is not usually fatal.

CHAPTER FIVE

Rogue Waves and Lost Ships

ROGUE WAVES

IN JULY 1895, AT WHAT MOST PEOPLE WOULD PROBABLY CONSIDER MID-dle age, Joshua Slocum, 51 years old, sailed out of Halifax, Nova Scotia, in his 36-foot sloop *Spray*, a worn-out oyster boat that he had completely rebuilt himself (see figure 5.1). In 1898, 3 years and 46,000 miles later, he returned after having accomplished one of the greatest feats in maritime history: becoming the first person to single-handedly circumnavigate the entire globe. The account of his remarkable voyage, *Sailing Alone around the World*, became an instant best-seller. Surviving 46,000 miles of ocean sailing in a small sailboat alone is a mind-boggling accomplishment, especially in 1895 without satellite navigation, a cell phone, or any of our other modern technologies. While Slocum's voyage was an extraordinary achievement, early Polynesian sailors with their own navigation meth-ods, which seem very simple by today's standards, relying primarily on the constellations, managed to sail canoes across thousands of miles of Pacific Ocean to populate places like the Hawaiian Islands about 1,500 years ago.

Today, 125 years after Slocum's adventure, large ships, 20 or more times longer than the *Spray*, with all the modern navigation equipment available, sailing through the same oceans, have encountered rogue waves or some other aqueous obstacle and disappeared without a trace. Reported encounters with very large waves at sea from ship captains and crew were treated by oceanographers for years as exaggerations or simply the stories of sailors who had spent too much time at sea. There was no

Figure 5.1. Joshua Slocum seated on the cabin roof of *Spray*.
COURTESY OF THE NEW BEDFORD WHALING MUSEUM, WINFIELD SCOTT CLIME, CIRCA 1907.

shortage of these stories from survivors, and then there were the large number of ships, in many cases very large ships, that simply disappeared without leaving any evidence behind. And for oceanographers, who today have a number of sophisticated tools available to accurately document wave heights, these early accounts lacked any actual measurements to substantiate what seemed like outrageous or impossible claims (see figure 5.2). And scientists are scientists; they want proof.

One of the earliest accounts of an enormous wave took place in December 1942, on a stormy voyage across the Atlantic from New York City to the British Isles. In the early days of World War II, Prime Minister Winston Churchill had offered President Franklin Roosevelt two luxury liners, the *Queen Mary* and the *Queen Elizabeth*, to speed up the delivery of badly needed American troops to Britain. These ships were the fastest ocean liners in existence at the time and could cross the Atlantic in just 5 days. Because of their speed, they could outrun or outmaneuver any German submarines. They were, in fact, a much safer way to get soldiers

Figure 5.2. The *Discoverer*, an NOAA research vessel, endures punishing waves in the Bering Sea off the coast of Alaska.
COURTESY OF COMMANDER RICHARD BEHN, NATIONAL OCEANIC AND ATMOSPHERIC ADMINISTRATION.

to Britain than conventional troop transports, and therefore, they didn't need a navy escort. Both ships were put into action and over the course of the war managed to move more than 765,000 troops across the North Atlantic, safely and without a single casualty.

Docked in New York, the *Queen Mary*, at 1,000 feet long, was significantly larger than the nearby US Navy destroyers and battleships (see figure 5.3).[1] There were more than 2,100 staterooms that slept eight soldiers on 12-hour shifts in order to transport as many men as possible (16,000 at a time). By the fourth day out of New York, however, a storm had developed, and the strong winds started to pitch and roll the liner around. The severe movement of the ship, in addition to the forces of the large waves and high winds, was in large part due to the *Queen Mary* carrying seven times as many passengers as normal, in addition to all the additional equipment, such as weapons and ammunition. This combined

Figure 5.3.   The RMS *Queen Mary* arrives in New York harbor, June 20, 1945.
COURTESY OF THE US NAVY, PUBLIC DOMAIN, VIA WIKIMEDIA COMMONS.

to make her top heavy and even more prone to severe rolling (side-to-side movement of a ship). Additionally, the fuel oil was in tanks located below the waterline, so as more fuel was used, the top-heavy effect grew worse.

Much to the concern of the captain, crew, and soldiers, the winds soon reached hurricane force, and the overloaded ship shook as she climbed each wave crest and then disappeared into the next trough. By this time, hundreds of men were seasick, although the warning was clear that they were not to go near the railing to vomit, as it was a 65-foot drop to the water from the main deck, and the ship wasn't going to stop and look for a lost man in these conditions. About 700 miles from Scotland, the *Queen Mary* slid down into what seemed like a bottomless trough and was then hit on the port (left) side by a massive wave that was at least twice as high as any they had yet encountered. This mountain of water broke windows on the bridge, 95 feet above the waterline, and tore off all the lifeboats on the port side of the top deck. The impact of this huge wall of water also broke through a number of portholes, sending cold seawater pouring into hundreds of cabins.

The most frightening outcome of the impact of this huge wave was the force on the port side of the ship. It pushed her over to what was later determined to have been 52° from vertical, where she seemed to remain suspended, not sure whether to just keep going and completely roll over or right herself. She did swing back, although damage to the ship and soldiers was substantial. Broken arms and legs and the fear of seeing their companions being washed through the passageways in seawater were all too common. Had she completely rolled over, the *Queen Mary* would have likely gone to the bottom, with the loss of up to 16,500 lives, becoming the biggest maritime disaster of all time. It would also have easily become the greatest maritime mystery of all time, having disappeared without an SOS call or any evidence left at the surface. The officers on the bridge were fortunately able to swing the ship to face into the swell, which likely saved them all from total disaster.

As odd as it may seem, just 2 months later, in February 1943, the *Queen Mary*'s sister ship, the *Queen Elizabeth*, also loaded with troops, went through essentially an identical near disaster when hit with a wave described as twice as large as the others they were plowing through on their way to the British Isles. The wave washed up high enough to damage guns on the exposed forward deck and shattered the windows on the bridge 92 feet above the waterline. While damaged, the *Elizabeth* also made it to her destination.

Because of the war, the reporting and significance of these two encounters didn't reach oceanographers right away, but when discovered, it led to the first description and naming of these mammoth walls of water as *rogue waves*. As it turns out, there have now been many similar events documented. There have also been a number of large ships that have disappeared completely, often without a shred of evidence left behind, which has begun to confirm the existence of anomalously large waves.

While oceanographers have become pretty proficient at determining which wind conditions (speed, duration, and fetch) will produce which size of waves hundreds of miles away, rogue waves are a completely different beast that have defied prediction. Reaching up to 100 feet in height and completely unexpected, these beasts have broken large oil tankers in half and disabled cruise ships.

As more encounters with these rogue waves began to be reported, scientists started to recognize a connection between very large waves and ocean currents. Oceanographers using mathematical models have shown how energy can be passed from an ocean current to waves moving in the opposite direction from the current. Near the Cape of Good Hope at the southern tip of Africa, for example, the Agulhas Current has been implicated in a number of rogue waves where it interacts with large Southern Ocean swells. The waters between South Africa and Antarctica form a continuous band around Antarctica, known as the roaring forties because this zone is south of 40° latitude. One of the three properties of winds that produce waves is fetch, or the distance the wind blows over the sea surface. Everything else being equal, which it rarely is, the greater the fetch, the larger the waves. Because there are no continents at this latitude, wind can blow great distances and generate very large waves, which often makes passage to Antarctica or getting around the Cape of Good Hope or Cape Horn treacherous for ships.

On June 13, 1968, a 737-foot-long supertanker, the *World Glory*, with 334,000 barrels of Kuwait crude oil, was working its way around the Cape of Good Hope. While tankers usually used a safer and shorter route through the Suez Canal, it had been closed by the Arab-Israeli War, so they were forced to take the longer and often more dangerous route. The *World Glory* was heading into large waves but managing these until about three o'clock in the afternoon, when the officers on the bridge noticed a much larger wave approaching. The bow buried itself into the wave, which then moved under the middle of the tanker, lifting her high in the air and leaving both the bow and the stern suspended and unsupported. The weight of 334,000 barrels of oil in both the bow and the stern bent the ship and left a crack across the main deck. The motion of the ship opened and closed the crack, much like you can bend an aluminum

Figure 5.4. The *World Glory* off the Cape of Good Hope after being broken in half.
COURTESY OF UNKNOWN, WITH ACKNOWLEDGMENT TO HTTP://THEPOWEROFTHESEA.COM/IMAGES.
HTML.

can back and forth to twist it in half, but this was a 737-foot-long steel container filled with crude oil. Another large wave lifted the bow again and then let it drop, which ripped the ship totally in half (see figure 5.4). Both bow and stern remained afloat for several hours with oil pouring out, some of it catching fire, until the waves put out the flames. The 34 crew members were now split between the two separate halves. Only 10 of the crew were rescued. Based on the captain's observations, it was believed that the wave that broke the ship's back was at least 70 feet high.

In February 1995, the *Queen Elizabeth II* encountered what was described as a 95-foot wall of water, also in the North Atlantic. The ship's captain said it "came out of the darkness" and "looked like the White Cliffs of Dover." He was able to determine the wave's height because the crest was level with the ship's bridge. The wave broke over the bow with explosive force and smashed many of the windows and part of its forward deck.

Two cruise ships that take tourists across the South Atlantic to Antarctica, the MS *Bremen* and the *Caledonian Star*, collided with rogue waves nearly 100 feet high within a week and 600 miles of each other in early 2001. Both vessels had their bridge windows broken, and the *Bremen* drifted without navigation or propulsion for 2 hours. The first officer of the *Caledonian Star* stated that it was "just like a mountain, a wall of water coming against us."

In April 2005, the *Norwegian Dawn*, a cruise ship with 2,500 passengers onboard, encountered rough seas between Miami and New York City, including three 70-foot-high waves. Windows were smashed on the 9th and 10th decks, and 60 cabins were flooded, although damage otherwise was minor. This is not the kind of experience most people who sign up for ocean cruises are expecting, but once you get out into any ocean, conditions can change quickly, and calm seas are never guaranteed.

In March 2007, Holland America's cruise ship MS *Prinsendam* was hit by a 70-foot-high wave in the Antarctic part of a voyage around the tip of South America. This was actually MS *Prinsendam* number 2, as the first sank off Alaska in October 1980 and is described later in this chapter.

These cruise ships and their passengers were lucky in experiencing very large waves, and in all cases, they survived relatively undamaged. Other ships have not been as fortunate. The German container ship MS *München* left Bremerhaven, Germany, on a cold day in late 1978 headed for Savannah, Georgia (see figure 5.5). On December 12, the ship, two and a half football fields long and described as unsinkable, vanished with a single unintelligible distress call. All that was found in a wide search of

Figure 5.5.   The container ship MS *München*.
COURTESY OF HAPAG-LLOYD AG, HAMBURG, GERMANY.

the general area was some scattered debris and an unlaunched lifeboat that was originally secured on the deck 65 feet above the water line (see figure 5.6). Its attachment pins had been "twisted as though hit by an extreme force." The best guess at the time was that the ship had been struck by a very large wave.

The unexplained loss of a vessel carrying out ocean research in the Hawaiian Islands touched me 42 years ago. We were recruiting an oceanographer/ocean engineer to join our faculty at the University of California, Santa Cruz. Our preferred candidate, Gary Niemeyer, was an assistant professor of ocean engineering at the University of Hawaii and looked like a perfect fit for our young group.

On the afternoon of December 9, 1978, Niemeyer and nine colleagues departed from Honolulu for the second of six planned 6-day cruises to support the development of an ocean thermal energy conversion (OTEC) project at Ke-ahole Point, Hawaii. Two days later, on

Figure 5.6.   The only surviving part of the MS *München*, a single lifeboat covered with barnacles.
COURTESY OF HAPAG-LLOYD AG, HAMBURG, GERMANY.

December 11, the 92-foot vessel *Holoholo* failed to arrive at Kawaihae Harbor on the Big Island as scheduled. The total distance between the two harbors was only about 150 miles, and the disappearance of the vessel led to a search-and-rescue operation involving the US Coast Guard, the navy and air force, Coast Guard auxiliary, Civil Air Patrol, and the University of Hawaii. More than 520 flight hours were spent covering 377,000 square miles of ocean—equivalent to the combined areas of California, Oregon, and Nevada—with no success.

There were just two bits of evidence that were ever recovered, and one of these was uncertain. The first was on December 17, 8 days after the *Holoholo* left Honolulu, and was a wooden box that held a current meter and was known to be onboard the vessel. A fisherman found the box floating about 55 miles off the southwest coast of Hawaii. There had been no distress call or radio message; nothing was ever recovered but a floating instrument box. The second was a photograph taken by a high-altitude U-2 aircraft flight on December 18 showing a vessel—possibly the *Holoholo*—at a location about 82 miles off the southwest coast of Hawaii, in the same general vicinity of the current meter box.

After months of investigations, hearings, testimony, and litigation focused on the tragic loss of life and disappearance of the *Holoholo*, the conclusions reached in both the National Transportation Safety Board Marine Accident Report and the Department of Transportation Coast Guard Marine Casualty Report were essentially the same:

- The *Holoholo* was a converted pleasure boat and was in an unseaworthy condition for the intended voyage as a result of two deck openings that had their metal hatches removed and replaced by plywood covers. In rough seas, waves penetrating these covers would have allowed rapid internal flooding of the rudder and then the engine compartments, followed by capsizing.

- Weather conditions at sea deteriorated during the cruise, and by December 10, the forecast was for strong, gusty trade winds to 30 knots and seas at 12 feet. A vessel in the vicinity on that same day reported 20-foot seas. Sea conditions did not improve, and this period was later described as one of the longest intervals of continuous gale-force winds in recent history.

- The Coast Guard report acknowledged that the exact cause of the casualty was unknown but, based on all available information, concluded that the "casualty occurred on 10 December 1978 during the afternoon or evening. Significant wave heights (the average of the highest one-third of the waves) at the probable time/place of the casualty were 14–17.5 feet with occasional wave heights of 22.4–28 feet."

- "The primary cause of the casualty was determined to be ingress of water in heavy seas and possible progressive flooding. This may have started with ingress into the steering gear compartment through the compromised (non-watertight) 2' × 4' opening left by the earlier removal of the fantail deck hatch. Alternatively, the casualty might have been caused by the slamming force of *Holoholo* trying to make headway into heavy seas. The heavy pitching combined with the vessel's flat bottom might have provided unusually high stresses in critical areas of the main deck. A structural fracture of this sort, however, should have produced additional debris."

- Regardless of the primary cause, the reports concluded that the loss was immediate and catastrophic, which precluded radio distress calls, signaling, deployment of life rafts or other life-saving operations.

The investigation and information gathered in the weeks and months following the loss of the *Holoholo* was far more extensive than for most lost ships, and despite all the data collected, it cannot be said with certainty exactly what happened to the ship and why it disappeared without a trace. Was it the combined impacts of a number of large waves on a compromised ship, or the impacts of one very large wave? We will likely never know.

In 1995, an oil platform in the North Sea with a wave gauge measured a single rogue wave with a height of 84 feet for the first time. A similar wave-measuring system using a laser had been deployed on a bridge connecting two production oil platforms in the Danish sector of the North Sea and had been in operation from 1981 through 1993. When this 12-year record was carefully analyzed in 1997, at least 446 rogue waves were identified (see figure 5.7). Other data sets were also evaluated and led to the finding that many rogue waves had been edited out of the data because they were considered "instrument errors."

The increasing incidence of these anomalously large waves led to the initiation of a 5-year project by the European Space Agency in 2000 to look into how common rogue waves might actually be and if they might explain the losses of at least some of these large ships. With twin satellites that used radar to observe waves at the sea surface, scientists initially evaluated 30,000 images for a 3-week period when the *Bremen* and the *Caledonian Star* were damaged. Even though this was a brief period of

Figure 5.7.   Large waves battering the Borgholm Dolphin, an oil platform in the Irish Sea.
COURTESY OF RICHARD CHILD, CC BY 2.0 VIA FLICKR.

time, the team of scientists identified 10 giant waves from around the world that were more than 80 feet in height! This came as a big surprise and provided compelling evidence that large rogue waves are far more common than previously believed and not just the result of sailor's imaginations.

This initial series of observations also revealed that these giant waves often occur where ordinary wind waves encounter ocean currents. The strength of the current seems to concentrate the wave energy, much like a lens concentrates light. These conditions normally occur far out to sea, however, so no need to worry excessively about rogue waves attacking you on the beach.

In the 20 years between 1981 and 2001, 124 ships more than 600 feet long were reported to have sunk at sea, often by what is usually called "severe weather." That's a large ship lost every 2 months! But the most recent estimates of the total number of large merchant ships indicate that there are about 50,000 of these around the globe. Like many other potential hazards on the high seas, and despite the accounts described here, the probability of sinking is very low; 6 ships lost each year of 50,000 ships at sea is a very small number.

I have been fortunate to have twice taught the Semester at Sea program, where a 500-foot cruise ship sails around the world with 600 college students on a three-and-a-half-month voyage of discovery. Classes are held every day while at sea, and there are frequent port calls with educational and travel experiences and opportunities. I also taught on a shorter 2-month voyage across the Pacific and back. While there were occasional stormy days, which made teaching challenging, I never felt that I was in a dangerous or hazardous situation.

OTHER DANGERS TO SHIPS AT SEA

There are other dangers to ships at sea, however, in addition to the occasional 90-foot-high rogue wave. John August Shedd wrote in 1928, "A ship in a harbor is safe, but that is not what ships are built for." In fact, it's been said that the only difference between being on a ship and being in prison is that you can't drown in prison.

One of the most widely publicized peacetime nautical disasters of all time, the RMS *Titanic* sank on her maiden voyage from Southampton to New York City in the early-morning hours of April 15, 1912 (see figures 5.8 and 5.9). Of the 1,320 passengers and 892 crew, more than 1,500 died, including the captain and the chief naval architect of the vessel, after the ship hit an iceberg south of Newfoundland.

The *Titanic* carried some of the wealthiest people in the world, as well as hundreds of emigrants from Great Britain, Ireland, Sweden, Italy, Syria, and Russia who were searching for a better life in the United States. At 882 feet long, she was the largest ship afloat at the time she embarked on her first voyage. This ship was as luxurious as any ocean liner ever constructed, with lavish first-class staterooms, a swimming pool, a gymnasium, libraries, and elegant restaurants.

Figure 5.8.   The RMS *Titanic* nearly ready for launch.
COURTESY OF ROBERT JOHN WELCH (1859–1936), OFFICIAL PHOTOGRAPHER FOR HARLAND & WOLFF, PUBLIC DOMAIN, VIA WIKIMEDIA COMMONS.

Figure 5.9. The RMS *Titanic* departing Southampton.
COURTESY OF UNKNOWN, PUBLIC DOMAIN, VIA WIKIMEDIA COMMONS.

Although a number of sophisticated safety features had been designed into the ship, including separate watertight compartments and remotely operated watertight hatches, it carried only enough lifeboats for about half of the people onboard. Lax maritime safety regulations at that time allowed for this deficiency. The lifeboat capacity was based on the belief that the most likely scenario for evacuation was that passengers would be taken off the ship to some nearby rescue vessel. The lifeboats could, therefore, make multiple trips so that there wasn't a need for boats for the entire number of passengers. Were the passengers aware of this, or did the potential for a disaster even enter their minds as they boarded the "unsinkable" luxury vessel? What was the likelihood in a 3,200-mile voyage across the Atlantic that there was going to be another ship nearby to take on any passengers in the event of a major disaster?

Four days into the crossing, the ship received six warnings of sea ice on the day of the collision from other vessels in the area. While running at full speed through a field of large icebergs was subsequently criticized as reckless, the practice then made staying on schedule for arrival the highest priority. Lookouts were onboard to keep a watch for icebergs, and although the crew on the bridge sighted the iceberg, at a vessel speed of 22 knots (about 25 miles per hour), she couldn't turn fast enough to avoid hitting it. On April 14, 1912, and 375 miles south of Newfoundland, the *Titanic* made impact at 11:40 p.m.

While the ship was able to turn and avoid a head-on collision, the glancing blow buckled a number of steel hull plates along about 300 feet of her starboard (right) side. Icy seawater immediately began flowing into 6 of her 16 watertight compartments at an estimated rate of 1,700 gallons per second, 15 times faster than it could have been pumped out. The ship was designed to stay afloat with four of her compartments flooded, but not six. At 5 minutes after midnight, 25 minutes after the collision with the iceberg, the crew realized that the ship couldn't stay afloat with this damage and fired flares and sent radio messages to attract help. The captain ordered the ship's lifeboats uncovered and the passengers notified. Within 45 minutes of the impact, about 3,360,000 gallons of water, or the equivalent of six Olympic-size swimming pools, had already entered the *Titanic*.

At this point, the warnings and assistance provided to passengers varied depending on their class. First-class stewards only had a few passengers to assist, so they helped them get dressed and led them onto the main deck. Stewards for second- and third-class had many more people to deal with and essentially just opened cabin doors and told occupants to put on lifebelts and come on deck. Many passengers refused to believe anything serious was taking place and didn't want to leave the warmth of their cabins. There was no public address system at the time, so these passengers weren't told that the ship was sinking.

Things from this time until the ship sank at 2:20 a.m., 2 hours and 40 minutes after hitting the iceberg, went anything but smoothly for a variety of reasons. Although the *Titanic* was designed to carry 68 lifeboats, she only carried 20; 16 of these were wooden boats on davits, and the other four were collapsible boats with wooden bottoms and canvas sides. Two of these were stored upside down and had to be erected and carried to the davits to be launched. The other two were lashed on top of the officer quarters. These collapsible boats weighed several tons each, so moving them to the boat deck was a challenge under the existing conditions. Each of the larger wooden boats was designed to carry 68 passengers, which if filled to capacity would still have left more than 1,000 people on the vessel.

The lack of crew preparation, planning, and experience soon became apparent. There had been no lifeboat or fire drills since the ship left Southampton, which would be unheard of on any passenger ship today, where lifeboat drills occur with great regularity. While sailing on the SS *Universe* and *Universe Explorer* on the Semester at Sea program, we had lifeboat drills at least once a week (see figure 5.10). All passengers were ordered to dress as if they were going to abandon ship, put on their life-jackets, and report to their designated lifeboat stations for roll call. Typically, several lifeboats were lowered off the side to make sure they were functional, and the crew knew how to launch and operate them. This was all taken very seriously by the captain and the crew.

Figure 5.10.   Two of the author's daughters ready for a life raft drill in the Pacific on the Semester at Sea's SS *Universe*.
COURTESY OF GARY GRIGGS © 1984.

While lists had been posted on the *Titanic* assigning crew members to individual lifeboat stations, few appeared to have read them or knew what to do in an emergency. Many of the crew were not experienced seamen, and they were now faced with the challenge of lowering 20 boats full of people 70 feet down the sides of the ship, which was now slowly starting to list, or tilt, on a very cold dark night.

While the order was given to let women and children board the lifeboats first, the first two boats were lowered with just 28 passengers each, as there were no more women or children waiting. So rather than filling the remaining seats with the men standing by, the boats were lowered with many seats empty. Most of the passengers on the first lifeboats to be launched were from first or second class, as few third-class passengers had made it to the deck, having gotten lost on the lower levels or were trapped behind locked gates and partitions designed to segregate steerage passengers so they couldn't spread infectious diseases.

As the ship gradually tipped and then slipped beneath the water, hundreds of remaining crew and passengers jumped or slid into the icy water. At a temperature of 28°F, the water was lethally cold, and immersion into water of this temperature causes death within minutes from either cardiac arrest, cold incapacitation, or uncontrolled breathing of water. Almost all those who ended up in the water died of cardiac arrest or other reactions to the near-freezing water within 15 to 30 minutes. Only 13 survived by being helped into lifeboats, which could have carried nearly 500 additional people if they had been fully loaded (see figure 5.11).

While the RMS *Titanic* had luxury beyond belief, the preparation and readiness for an emergency was woefully inadequate, and more than 1,500 lives were lost as a result. Because of the passenger hierarchy, 97 percent of the first- and second-class children were saved, as were 93 percent of the first- and second-class women. Just 42 percent of the third-class women and children survived. But 82 percent of the male passengers and 78 percent of the crew lost their lives.

It should be mandatory today for any ship carrying passengers to have lifeboats and life vests for all onboard, and to conduct regular life-

Figure 5.11.   One of the partially filled *Titanic* lifeboats.
COURTESY OF UNKNOWN PASSENGER OF THE CARPATHIA, PUBLIC DOMAIN, VIA WIKIMEDIA
COMMONS.

boat drills so passengers know what to do and where to go in the event of an emergency.

A fire on a ship is always an unexpected and dangerous event, and when you are out at sea with no firefighters or fireboats around, it can potentially be disastrous. The original *Prinsendam* was a 427-foot-long cruise ship built in 1973 (see figure 5.12). She was in the Gulf of Alaska, about 120 miles south of Yakutat, when at midnight on October 4, 1980, a serious fire broke out in the engine room. Within an hour, the captain declared that the fire was out of control and sent out a distress call for immediate assistance. Aircraft, including a C-130 turbo prop maritime control aircraft, was dispatched immediately. Several Coast Guard cutters were also directed to head toward the burning ship, as was a 1,000-foot-long supertanker, the *Williamsburgh*.

At 6:30 the following morning, the captain of the *Prinsendam*, Cornelius Wabeke, gave the order that no captain wants to give: "Abandon

Figure 5.12.   The MS *Prinsendam* on fire prior to sinking in the Gulf of Alaska, 1980.
COURTESY OF SERGEANT RICHARD D. MCKEE, PUBLIC DOMAIN, VIA WIKIMEDIA COMMONS.

ship!" With only 15 passengers and 25 crew members left onboard, all the remaining crew and passengers managed to get safely off the ship and into the lifeboats, filling them to capacity, which is an amazing accomplishment. Within an hour, the *Williamsburgh* had reached the *Prinsendam*, and passengers and crew from the surrounding lifeboats were picked up by helicopter and began to be transferred to the supertanker. By midafternoon, a Coast Guard cutter had arrived, and those in critical condition were taken to Sitka, Alaska, for medical treatment. By nine o'clock that evening, there were still 20 passengers and 2 Air Force staff in a lifeboat that were missing. At about one o'clock in the morning, 18 hours after the ordeal had begun, the Coast Guard vessel spotted a flare from the lifeboat, and they were also rescued. When it was over, a near miracle had been accomplished: all of the passengers and the entire crew has been rescued without a single fatality or a single serious injury. Most maritime emergencies don't end this way, however.

On September 2, 2019, a 75-foot dive boat, the MV *Conception*, caught fire in the middle of the night while anchored near Santa Cruz Island about 24 miles off the coast of Santa Barbara. International and federal regulations require that vessels over a certain size be constructed of fire-resistant materials and to have both smoke alarms and fire sprinklers wired into the boat's electronic system and also connected to the bridge. Given the *Conception*'s size (less than 100 tons), age (38 years old), and with fewer than 49 bunks, she was not covered by these regulations. When the fire occurred, the boat was believed to have been in compliance with all the appropriate regulations, and during the most recent Coast Guard inspection just 7 months earlier, there had not been any significant issues. The certificate of inspection for the boat required one crew member designated as a roving patrol at all times when the bunks below deck were occupied.

Access to the bunk area on the lower deck was through a forward staircase that descended from the galley area and also a small aft, or rear, escape hatch located above one of the bunks. Former dive passengers could only remember the stairway exit and couldn't recall if they had been made aware of the aft emergency escape hatch. Both exits, however, appeared to have been blocked by the fire during the disaster.

About 3:00 a.m. on the night of the fire, there were 33 scuba divers and one crew member asleep below deck. One of the crew sleeping in the crew quarters on the upper deck was wakened by a pop that he thought was a disoriented passenger or one of the crew. He got up to see if he could help and quickly discovered an out-of-control fire in the galley, which had already spread to the aft end of the upper, or sun, deck and engulfed the ladder down to the main deck. He woke the four other crew members on the upper deck and placed a mayday call at 3:15 a.m. from the wheelhouse. Without a ladder, they had to jump to the main deck, leaving one member with a broken leg. Although they tried to access the main deck cabin (where the galley was located) through a forward window, the flames and smoke made it impossible. Two of the crew jumped overboard, while the captain and two others managed to get an inflatable dinghy into the water. They all got into the dinghy and paddled 200 yards to the closest boat anchored nearby.

Boats and helicopters from the Coast Guard and Santa Barbara and Ventura County fire departments were sent to the site, but the *Conception* was drifting into shallow water because the anchor line had been severed by the fire, which made trying to extinguish the fire from other vessels more difficult. The fire on the *Conception* was put out by 5:23 a.m. after having burned the vessel down to the waterline (see figure 5.13). Not long afterward, the boat sank in 64 feet of water about 60 feet from the north shore of Santa Cruz Island. All 33 dive passengers and one crew member died in the fire; the other five crew escaped with injuries.

Investigations and inquiries concluded that the company running the dive boat was a respectable business. This fire was the only one that locals remembered, and it wasn't an issue that the local industry contemplated. While it's always difficult to know the cause of a fire when destruction is so total, the most likely source is a very large number of rechargeable devices, cell phones, cameras, and dive lights that may have overloaded circuits, coupled with the hazards of lithium-ion battery overloading. These are not typical concerns on any boat, but this was the most logical conclusion reached by the investigators.

This was certainly a tragedy, especially for my own community, as many of the divers were from the Santa Cruz and San Francisco Bay areas. Each disaster of any kind is often followed by new rules, regula-

Figure 5.13.   The dive boat *Conception* following the disastrous fire off Santa Cruz Island.
COURTESY OF THE NATIONAL TRANSPORTATION SAFETY BOARD, PUBLIC DOMAIN, VIA WIKIMEDIA COMMONS.

tions, and standards to reduce the risk of such events in the future. There are risks involved in many of our day-to-day activities, however, and we can never totally eliminate them from our lives. Being aware of the safety or dangers in our surroundings or activities, and knowing as much as can be known about how to respond in an emergency, are commonsense recommendations, especially on a boat out of sight of land.

Note

1. Many of the accounts discussed here come from Bruce Parker's well-researched book *The Power of the Sea: Tsunamis, Storm Surges, Rogue Waves, and Our Quest to Predict Disasters* (New York: Palgrave Macmillan, 2012).

CHAPTER SIX

The Bermuda Triangle

Where Ships and Planes Go to Disappear

THERE ARE THOSE PLACES, THOSE STORIES, THOSE UNEXPLAINED MYS-
teries that have captured our imagination and kept it for years—Roswell,
New Mexico, and UFOs; Big Foot and yeti; the lost continent of Atlantis;
and the Bermuda Triangle, among others. These seemingly unexplained
phenomena have spawned dozens of books, more than a few movies,
museums, and even cults who have absolutely no question in their minds
about the reality of these incidents that just can't be explained.

The Bermuda Triangle, also sometimes referred to as the Devil's Triangle and Hurricane Alley, is a somewhat mythical section of the Atlantic
Ocean enclosed in a triangle between Florida, Bermuda, and Puerto Rico
(see figure 6.1). The first mention of this roughly 500,000-square-mile
piece of ocean goes back at least as far as 1952, when there was a story in
Fate magazine—which for more than 70 years has covered the strange,
unknown, and paranormal—about what appeared to be a large number
of unexplained incidents in the area. Other articles, books, and even a
documentary (*The Devil's Triangle*) followed. The basis of the stories
stems from ships and planes that were purported to have mysteriously
disappeared in this swath of sea, swallowed up without a trace.

Some of the most cited events took place 75 to more than 100 years
ago, when weather reports, navigation equipment, and communication
systems were pretty primitive by today's standards. Many of the early
stories and accounts were written 40 or 50 years ago, often many years

Figure 6.1. Geographic extent of the Bermuda Triangle.
COURTESY OF THE NATIONAL OCEANIC AND ATMOSPHERIC ADMINISTRATION, VIA FLICKR.

after the original incidents. According to some more recent investigations, few of the early writers attempted to do any original research but used the information provided by earlier authors, who had done the same. Mistakes and fabrications continued to be repeated and reinforced and, in some cases, exaggerated.

The first disappearance that sowed the seeds of the Bermuda Triangle mystery took place in 1918—more than a century ago—when the biggest ship in the US Navy at the time, bizarrely named the USS *Cyclops*, was lost somewhere between Barbados and Baltimore (see figure 6.2). The *Cyclops* was indeed large for the time, nearly 550 feet long—almost two football fields—and had a crew of 306 men, along with 11,000 tons of manganese ore onboard. The ship left Brazil with the ore and then made a port call in Barbados to resupply for the voyage to Baltimore. The last recorded message was "Weather fair, all well."

But on the 9-day journey, something happened, and no trace of the ship or its crew were ever found. Although there are many ideas about what happened—storms, capsizing, wartime enemy activity (World War I, the "war to end all wars," was underway)—there is no clear evidence

Figure 6.2. The USS *Cyclops* before her disappearance.
COURTESY OF THE HARRIS AND EWING COLLECTION, LIBRARY OF CONGRESS, PRINTS AND PHOTO-
GRAPHS DIVISION.

because the ship was never found. However, two of *Cyclops*'s sister ships, *Proteus* and *Nereus*, were both transporting heavy loads of metallic ore similar to the *Cyclops* when they were lost in the North Atlantic during World War II. In all three cases, the ships are thought to have sunk due to structural failure resulting from overloading with much denser cargo than the ships were designed for.

While the sinking of the USS *Cyclops* remains a mystery, it could have happened anywhere between Barbados and Baltimore, a distance of more than 2,000 miles, and not necessarily in the famed Triangle. While proponents of the Bermuda Triangle phenomenon point to the lack of a distress call as evidence of something very strange, the truth is that in 1918, wireless communication was pretty unreliable, and it wouldn't have been at all unlikely for a rapidly sinking vessel not to have had time to send a successful distress call before sinking. Recently, many ships passing through these waters have observed very large or rogue waves 70 feet in height, so the *Cyclops* encountering a very large wave somewhere along this 2,000-mile trip is certainly a reasonable explanation for its disappearance.

In 1963, the SS *Marine Sulphur Queen*, an oil tanker that had been converted to carry molten sulfur, disappeared off the southern coast of Florida with its crew of 39 (see figure 6.3). No trace of the ship or the crew was ever located. While this mysterious loss is often included in books about the Triangle, the authors don't usually mention that the US Coast Guard had reported that the *Sulphur Queen* was in appalling condition and should never have gone to sea to begin with. Fires apparently erupted with regularity onboard, and the ship also possessed what was referred to as a "weak back," meaning that the keel could split when weakened by corrosion, causing the ship to break in half. The conversion from an oil tanker to a ship carrying molten sulfur gave the vessel a very high center of gravity, adding to the probability of capsizing. It seems

Figure 6.3.   The SS *Marine Sulphur Queen.*
COURTESY OF THE US COAST GUARD.

that this ship was a floating disaster, and its loss cannot simply be blamed on the Bermuda Triangle.

The unexplained disappearance of Flight 19, in particular, fueled the flames of the Bermuda Triangle mystery. On December 5, 1945, five US Navy Grumman TBM Avenger torpedo bombers took off from the naval air station in Fort Lauderdale, Florida, on what was to be a 2-hour training mission over the Atlantic (see figures 6.4 and 6.5). After losing radio contact with their base, all five planes and their 14 crew members vanished without a trace. One of the early Triangle books suggests that the patrol disappeared in ideal flight conditions, but a closer investigation revealed it wasn't fine weather at all; rather, there were waves nearly 50 feet in height in the Atlantic below them. The only truly experienced pilot in the mission was its leader, Lieutenant Charles Taylor, and his error appears to have played a part in the tragedy that unfolded.

The plan for Flight 19 was to head east from the naval air station to conduct a practice bombing run, then fly over Grand Bahama Island, and then turn southwest and return home. Along the way Lieutenant Taylor became confused when his compass apparently failed, and he thought that the planes were moving in the wrong direction. Taylor instructed the planes to fly northeast, thinking that he was heading toward Florida; instead, they were heading farther out into the Atlantic.

At some point, "as the planes [flew] closer to the Bermuda Triangle," their radio signals started to fade. Eventually, communication was lost, and the five planes with their 14 crew members disappeared. The lost planes became a legend, particularly after 1964, when an article, "The Deadly Bermuda Triangle" by Vincent Gaddis, was published in *Argosy* magazine, not usually recognized for its science reporting. Gaddis was an American author who named the Bermuda Triangle and popularized a number of stories about anomalous and paranormal phenomena, which have been criticized by skeptics for being inaccurate and misleading and for ignoring possible natural explanations and inventing mysteries where none existed. Gaddis wrote, "Whatever menace that lurks within the triangle of a tragedy so close to home . . . was responsible for the most incredible mystery in the history of aviation—the lost patrol."

Figure 6.4.   One of the deadly aerial torpedoes carried by the US Navy's crack torpedo bomber, the Grumman Avenger.
COURTESY OF THE DEPARTMENT OF DEFENSE, NATIONAL ARCHIVES.

Figure 6.5. Grumman Avengers flying in formation.
COURTESY OF LIEUTENANT COMMANDER HORACE BRISTOL, US NAVY, PUBLIC DOMAIN, VIA WIKI-
MEDIA COMMONS.

A more recent and careful investigation of the "lost patrol" uncovered some interesting history of Lieutenant Charles Taylor: "[He] arrived with a hangover, flew off without a watch, and had a history of getting lost and ditching his plane twice before." While Lieutenant Taylor was an experienced pilot, he hadn't spent a lot of time flying over the Bahamas where he was intending to head on the patrol that day. How he got so confused right off the bat thinking he was heading south toward the Florida Keys instead of east toward the Bahamas isn't clear, but it was soon to determine the outcome of Flight 19's five planes and 14 men.

Communication records from the patrol before it vanished made it clear that Flight 19 had become unsure of its location, or at least that Lieutenant Taylor had become confused. The flight transcripts indicate that Taylor thought his compass had malfunctioned and that he believed he was above the Florida Keys, a string of low islands stretching southwest off the tip of Florida. Ground staff at the naval air station would subsequently reveal that they were actually to the southeast over an island in the Bahamas. At this point, Lieutenant Taylor overruled a junior pilot who said they should turn west; Taylor insisted that the patrol continue to fly east, taking them further out into the Atlantic.

Today all planes have global positioning systems (GPS) that communicate with orbiting satellites so that very accurate positions are known. As long as a pilot has a reliable and operational GPS system and knows how to use it, getting lost has a very low probability of occurring. In 1945, however, to locate a position over water, a pilot would need to know their starting point and how fast, how long, and in what direction they had flown. If an error was made in any of those numbers, then the pilot and plane were lost. There were no landmarks in the open ocean to navigate from.

By 4:45 p.m., it had become clear to the ground crew that Lieutenant Taylor was completely lost, and he was urged to turn over flight control to one of his students, which he apparently didn't do. As night fell, communications deteriorated, and it was evident that the patrol was still heading northeast, further out into the Atlantic. At 6:04 p.m., Taylor was overheard radioing to his crew, "All planes close up tight. . . . We'll have to ditch unless landfall. . . . When the first plane drops below 10 gallons, we all go down together." Although several search planes were sent out, there was never any sign of the planes or crews. With their fuel exhausted, they would have gone into the sea in a storm with 50-foot waves. These planes were heavy (14,000 pounds when empty) and were infamously nicknamed Iron Birds. When they hit the ocean, they would have sunk quickly into water thousands of feet deep.

Two Martin Mariner planes took off later that evening to search for the missing Avengers, although there was little hope at this point of finding the five missing planes, as they would likely have run out of fuel by then. The flight plan was for these two planes to meet over the search area. One of the Mariners, PBM-5 BuNo 59225, from Naval Air Station Banana River (now Patrick Air Force Base), took off into the winter night at 7:27 p.m. with 13 crewmen aboard. Within a few minutes, BuNo 59225 sent a routine message reporting its position and gave no hint of any problems with their plane. There were no more recorded messages.

Less than 2 hours later, at 9:15 p.m., a passing oil tanker, the SS *Gaines Mills*—which had no connection with any of the military planes but was on a routine voyage—reported seeing a midair explosion at 28.59°N, 80.25°W, followed by flames 100 feet high burning on the sea surface for about 10 minutes. This observation is believed to mark the midair explosion of BuNo 59225, which stopped responding to radio messages and disappeared at that same time. Despite heading at full speed to the likely crash site and conducting a thorough search for survivors, the SS *Gaines Mills* found no traces of the Mariner or any of its crew. Another account of this incident, however, stated that the search was conducted in a pool of oil and debris.

Some of the follow-up stories on what now became the sixth disappearing plane claim that the PBM Mariner was known to experience vapor leaks when fully loaded with fuel, which led aircrews to label the plane the "flying gas tank." The fact that the plane disappeared off the radar at the same time as the sighting of the fireball led to the most logical explanation that, true to its undesirable reputation, BuNo 59225 exploded midflight. Speculation was that one of the crew onboard (sometimes listed as 13 and sometimes as 22 men), unaware of the gas fumes in the unpressurized cabin, may have lit a cigarette, leading to the explosion. At the earliest light the next morning, December 6, 1945, the US Navy sent out a reported 300 ships and aircraft to search for both Flight 19 and the PBM Mariner. For 5 days, they searched over land and water but found no sign of oil slicks, wreckage, or any bodies. Fortunately, no more rescue vessels vanished.

Recent investigators have looked more carefully at some of the mysterious disappearances of ships and planes and discovered that while popular writers had stated that a ship or plane had disappeared in "calm seas," actual records showed a raging storm had been underway. Other descriptions reported that ships had "mysteriously vanished" when their remains had actually been found and the cause of their sinking explained. In one odd case, a ship listed as missing in the Bermuda Triangle had been lost some 3,000 miles away in the Pacific Ocean. The writer had confused the name of the Pacific port the ship had departed from with a city of the same name on the Atlantic coast.

There is no question that this swath of ocean has had a large number of marine disasters, but it is also one of the busiest sections of ocean in the world. Large numbers of commercial ships and small boats cross through it, and airliners and military and private aircraft fly over this area in great numbers. The waters in this region are also not known for their year-round calmness, with summer bringing frequent hurricanes and the warm waters of the Gulf Stream capable of initiating sudden storms.

The maritime insurance company Lloyd's of London doesn't recognize this area of ocean as especially hazardous. For the insurance business, the ocean is a dangerous and somewhat unpredictable environment, no matter where you are at sea. The US Coast Guard reports that the number of supposed lost vessels is relatively insignificant considering the number of ships and aircraft that pass through this area of ocean regularly. In a random sampling from 1975, the US Seventh Coast Guard district reported that 21 ships disappeared without a trace in coastal waters off the United States—but only four of these disappeared in the Bermuda Triangle. With the waters off the southeast coast of the United States being among the busiest in the world with more than 150,000 vessels crossing through them every year and more than 10,000 calls for assistance, the Coast Guard has said that they're surprised that losses in the Triangle aren't even higher.

A *Nova* episode, "The Case of the Bermuda Triangle," that aired on June 27, 1976, was highly critical of the many magazine stories and sensational books on the topic. They stated, "When we've gone back to the original sources of the people involved, the mystery evaporates. Science does not have to answer questions about the Triangle because those questions are not valid in the first place. . . . Ships and planes behave in the Triangle the same way they behave everywhere else in the world."

Perhaps not surprisingly, the more recent investigations and explanations have not stopped the regular publications and stories claiming the losses and mysterious disappearances haven't been resolved by conventional scientific explanations. To counter the claims that para-normal, supernatural, or extraterrestrial activity are the causes of these disappearing ships and planes in the Bermuda Triangle, scientists have offered more rational explanations. Among the most frequent is simple human error. Pilots and sailors often go unprepared and poorly equipped for the conditions they are likely to encounter in an area known for its unpredictable weather. They often make navigational errors that can be catastrophic, which seems to have been the case with the five planes on Flight 19.

The offshore weather in the area can change quite rapidly, despite how idyllic it may seem while lying on a white sandy beach in Florida on a calm summer day. Hurricanes, tropical squalls, tropical storms with light-ning strikes, and atmospheric electrical disturbances can produce radio interference, anomalous compass readings, and equipment failures—all potential recipes for disaster for a plane or ship traversing this often-troubled area.

I end this chapter with a personal account of transit through this famed and often maligned area. In December 1984, my family and I were on the last leg of a 3-month around-the-world voyage on the SS *Universe* as part of the Semester at Sea program. We were on a course from Cadiz, Spain, to Ft. Lauderdale, Florida, where our voyage would end, and (you may have guessed) we were going to pass right through the Bermuda Triangle, which I hadn't given a thought to. After being on an older cruise ship for 3 months, you get used to constant noise and vibration. The SS *Universe* was shaking and noisy all the time, no matter where you were on the ship, day or night.

But late at night or very early in the morning the day before we were to land in Ft. Lauderdale, while most everyone was sleeping, the ship suddenly grew completely quiet and stopped vibrating. Perhaps most people slept more soundly than I did, but it was immediately obvious to me. The engines, the ventilation system, everything was deathly quiet. For perhaps a half-hour, this peace and calm persisted and was quite pleasant actually. And then the engines started up again, the noise and vibrations began, and we continued our voyage to Florida—and there was never any explanation I could find for why everything suddenly stopped. But fortunately, the captain and crew on the SS *Universe* had mandatory abandon-ship drills at least once a week. Everyone put on their life jackets and reported to our lifeboat stations for roll call. Fortunately, nothing ever happened on our voyage, but I felt we were prepared in case it did.

CHAPTER SEVEN

Hurricanes, Cyclones, and Typhoons

ON NOVEMBER 8, 2013, TYPHOON HAIYAN, ALSO KNOWN AS SUPER Typhoon Yolanda, the strongest tropical cyclone ever (based on wind velocities) to make landfall, cut a devastating swath across the central Philippines in the western tropical Pacific. The storm strength was equivalent to a category 5 hurricane (the highest level of intensity), with sustained wind speeds at landfall of 195 miles per hour, the highest ever recorded, and gusts up to 235 miles per hour. Nobody is standing outside in winds this powerful; when wind speed reaches about 120 miles per hour, it is no longer possible for a human being to stand up. Nearly 13 million people were affected by Yolanda, 13 percent of the nation's population. There were at least 6,300 fatalities and 28,700 injuries. Because of the lightweight construction materials commonly used in the Philippines and the extreme wind velocities, more than 281,000 houses were destroyed, with 1.9 million people displaced.

This strong typhoon had been closely tracked for 6 days across the western Pacific as its strength increased prior to slamming into the Philippines. As the storm intensified, evacuation warnings were given, including the highest level of warning, indicating very strong winds. Although wind speeds were extreme, the major cause of damage and loss of life appears to have been the storm surge. Water reached 17 feet above sea level at the center of the low-lying and most damaged area, Tacloban City (see figures 7.1 and 7.2), where the airport terminal building was destroyed when the surge reached the second floor. The entire first floor of the Tacloban City Convention Center, which was serving as an evac-

Figure 7.1.　Impact of Super Typhoon Haiyan (Yolanda) on Tacloban, Lyete Island, in the Philippines.

Figure 7.2.　Destruction caused by Super Typhoon Haiyan (Yolanda) in the city of Tacloban, Philippines, which took at least 6,300 lives in 2013.

uation shelter, was submerged by the storm surge. Many people in the building were surprised by the fast-rising waters and subsequently were injured or drowned.

The most immediate threats to survivors of this typhoon, like many similar events, in order of urgency, were (1) lack of safe drinking water; (2) lack of shelter; (3) untreated injuries and illnesses; (4) insufficient food; (5) lack of sanitation and personal hygiene items; and (6) shortage of household supplies, like fuel. Even with advance warnings, when a storm of this magnitude hits a nation with a densely populated, low-lying coastal area like the Philippines, where infrastructure is limited in places and construction is very lightweight, the damage, death, and injury toll is going to be high.

THE GREAT STORM OF 1900: GALVESTON, TEXAS

The deadliest natural disaster in the history of the United States was a massive hurricane that hit the shoreline at Galveston, Texas, on September 9, 1900, and took between 6,000 and 12,000 lives. In the late 1800s, Galveston was a boom town and enjoyed one of the highest per-capita incomes in the United States. The city's business district was called the "Wall Street of the Southwest," and their natural harbor was one of the busiest ports in the nation. The low-lying city had weathered many storms throughout its nearly 60 years of existence, and with their prosperity, the city residents had grown complacent, believing that any future storms would be no worse than those they had already experienced. This is not uncommon for cities and communities that have suffered a major disaster; they tend to forget the past and move on, thinking that such an event won't happen again or be any worse. Unfortunately, things can always be worse. The 100-year flood can be topped by the 200-year flood or even occur twice in a single year.

Galveston was built on a sandy barrier island with a maximum elevation of about 9 feet above sea level. The 1900 hurricane was accompanied by a storm surge, however, that raised water levels as much as 15 feet, which washed completely over the entire island's population of 38,000. The storm destroyed about 7,000 buildings, including 3,636 homes, and in addition to the lives lost, it left another 10,000 people homeless. In

Figure 7.3.   *Pittsburg Post* story about the Galveston hurricane in 1900.

Figure 7.4.   Destruction on Galveston Island from the hurricane of 1900.

short, the prosperous city known as the "Wall Street of the Southwest" was essentially destroyed (see figures 7.3 and 7.4).

THE FORMATION OF TROPICAL CYCLONES

Tropical cyclones in the North Atlantic, Caribbean, and eastern Pacific are known as hurricanes. In the Indian Ocean, the same type of severe storm is referred to as a monsoon, and in the western Pacific, China, Japan, the Philippines, and Australia, they are called typhoons. But these are all tropical cyclones, which are very large, warm, humid, rotating air masses. In order to be designated as a hurricane or typhoon, a tropical cyclone must generate wind speeds of at least 74 miles per hour. Cyclones that don't develop these high winds are known as tropical storms and tropical depressions, but they can change their status without warning as they more fully develop. Some of the most damaging tropical cyclones have occurred in Southeast Asia, where population densities in exposed, low-lying coastal areas are often very high, and many of the buildings are of lightweight construction.

Hurricanes have been responsible for more loss of life in the United States than any other natural hazard (see figure 7.5). While the western portion of the United States and Alaska worry from time to time about earthquakes, large and damaging seismic events occur far less often than hurricanes and generally affect much smaller areas, and average annual death tolls are considerably less (about 20 per year in the twentieth century). There has only been a single earthquake in the 245-year history of the United States where more than 200 people died: the great 1906 San Francisco earthquake and fire, where fatality estimates are around 3,000. While virtually every state in the United States experiences flooding, the exposure and risk from individual flood events is considerably less than for hurricanes, and average annual deaths are far fewer.

For the period from 1901 to 2016, more than 16,000 people in the United States died in individual hurricanes. While there are uncertainties about the number of fatalities for many of these events, especially the older and larger ones, it is likely that deaths are undercounted. However, this amounts to an average of 138 fatalities every year from hurricanes.

U.S. 2021 Billion-Dollar Weather and Climate Disasters

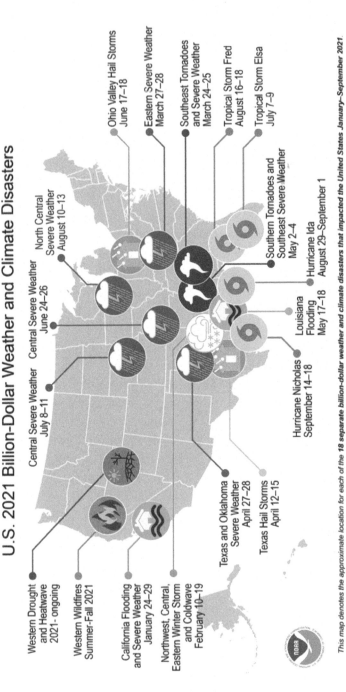

Figure 7.5. Billion-dollar weather and climate disasters for 2021.

COURTESY OF NOAA—NATIONAL CENTERS FOR ENVIRONMENTAL INFORMATION NCEI.

Sadly, while one death may be a tragedy in our own community, 1,000 deaths become a statistic.

While relatively harmless at sea—other than if you happen to be in a small boat far from shore—as these tropical cyclones approach land, their true impacts and potential for devastation and deaths are quickly realized. They routinely cause billions of dollars in damage and take hundreds of lives.

The official Atlantic hurricane season in the United States extends from June 1 to November 30 each year, but the peak usually occurs in August and September, when ocean-water temperatures are the highest. Warmer ocean water is a key factor in the formation of tropical cyclones because this is where they obtain their energy. Recent research suggests that there has been an increase in intense hurricane activity in the North Atlantic since the 1970s. While it isn't yet clear that there will be more hurricanes in the future, with a warming climate gradually leading to a warmer ocean, there will likely be more intense hurricanes along with higher wind velocities and greater rainfall. Between 1900 and 2006, 6 of the 10 most destructive hurricanes occurred in 2004 and 2005, and we can throw in Superstorm Sandy in 2012 on top of those. The 2020 Atlantic hurricane season was the most active on record, with 31 cyclones, all but one of which became a named storm. Of the 30 named storms, 13 developed into hurricanes, and 6 intensified into major hurricanes. It was only the second time in hurricane history in the United States that the number of named storms moved beyond the English alphabet and into Greek letters.

Although we tend to think of the Gulf and southern Atlantic coasts of the United States as the areas most exposed to hurricane damage, the paths of these tropical cyclones on occasion can reach as far north as New England, especially where areas like Long Island, Rhode Island, and Massachusetts extend into the Atlantic (see figures 7.6 and 7.7). About 60 million people today live in coastal counties that are vulnerable to hurricanes along the Gulf and southern Atlantic coasts, and like most coastal regions, these populations continue to increase, especially in people 65 and older, which has grown about 2 to 4 times faster than the total population.

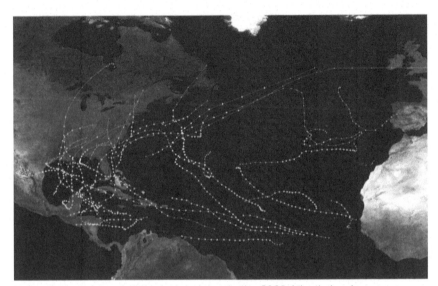

Figure 7.6. Tracks of all tropical cyclones in the 2020 Atlantic hurricane season. The individual points show the location of each storm at 6-hour intervals. Different shades of gray indicate different maximum sustained wind speeds. (The color represents the storm's maximum sustained wind speeds as classified in the Saffir-Simpson Hurricane Wind Scale.

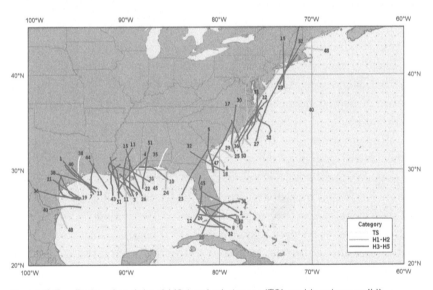

Figure 7.7. Paths of mainland US tropical storms (TS) and hurricanes (H) causing 25 or more deaths from 1851 to 2010.

From 1900 to 2015, there were 631 hurricanes that affected these counties and the Caribbean region, or 5.5 per year on average; 245 of these, or about 2.1 each year, have been classed as major hurricanes based on damage and death tolls. Most of these areas are known for their warm climates and sandy beaches and therefore have become magnets for retirees from the colder and more crowded upper Midwest and North Atlantic cities, even though hurricanes present a regular, predictable, and high risk to residents. Without some action to address the increasing concentrations of people and development in these coastal areas where hurricanes have historically made landfall, damage, injuries, and deaths will increase as more people, particularly less mobile, elderly people, choose to relocate to these areas.

Types of Hurricane Damage

Hurricane damage can be inflicted by the high-velocity winds (see figure 7.8), the impact of large storm waves, and the elevated sea levels and flooding, whether from storm surge (ocean water) or from high rainfall (freshwater runoff) that accompanies these tropical and subtropical cyclones. Structures engineered to withstand hurricane-force winds may well not have been designed to deal with flooding or submergence. In

Figure 7.8.   High-velocity wind damage in Byram, New Jersey, caused by Superstorm Sandy in 2012.
COURTESY OF WILLIAM JENNINGS, FEMA, NATIONAL ARCHIVES.

fact, very few if any homes are designed to withstand complete submergence. While Superstorm Sandy wasn't strictly classified as a hurricane, it made little difference when sea levels rose higher than ever recorded and flooded large sections of Manhattan.

Damage from Wind

Wind velocities during hurricanes start at 74 miles per hour, or the lower threshold for classification as a hurricane, and increase from there. Velocities commonly reach 150 miles per hour. The pressure exerted by the wind is proportional to the velocity squared, so a doubling of the wind speed produces 4 times as much force. As a result, the destructive power of high-velocity winds can literally blow structures over or apart, regardless of who is having an ill-planned hurricane party inside.

Wind generally produces much more damage than flooding, although once a roof is ripped off or windows are blown out, rain can enter a building and exacerbate the damage. There are many proven construction materials and methods that can help reduce wind damage: steeper roofs, eliminating overhanging eaves, concrete, metal, or tile roofs, laminated and tempered-glass windows, and strong shutters or plywood covers over windows. Nonetheless, during severe hurricanes with very high-velocity winds, all bets are off, and there are countless examples where entire oceanfront neighborhoods have been destroyed.

Storm Surge

The flooding of low-lying areas—including homes, businesses, and streets—during hurricanes is usually caused by the interaction of several processes, including storm surge (also often referred to as storm or hurricane tides, although they are unrelated to the tide) and large, breaking waves. High onshore wind velocities and low atmospheric pressures can allow the sea surface to rise along the shoreline, which in extreme cases may be an astounding 10 to 15 feet and, in the extreme, as high as 25 feet above normal predicted sea level. This is unheard of along the Pacific coast, where we may get very high tides or El Niños, usually at most a foot or two above predicted high-water levels.

In the great Galveston Island hurricane of 1900 (known also as Isaac's Storm, named after the local weatherman who tried to warn the city of the approaching hurricane), the storm surge reached nearly 15 feet above normal tides and washed completely over the island, which had an average elevation of about 9 feet above sea level. The city was completely unprepared and was nearly totally destroyed, as large wooden houses and other structures literally floated away into the Gulf of Mexico. The death toll, mainly from drowning, made it the deadliest natural disaster in US history. In rebuilding Galveston, sand and mud were pumped out of the bay to raise the elevation of part of the island 17 feet above its former elevation. A large seawall 21 feet high was built to provide protection for 10 miles of the eastern, more developed end of 30-mile-long Galveston Island (see figure 7.9). All protection ends somewhere, however, and the Galveston seawall does not protect the western end of the island or the inland side of the island from storm surge.

Hurricane Ike, 108 years later, passed directly over Galveston Island. The storm surge reached up to 20 feet above normal tide, 5.2 feet above the 1900 hurricane level, and overtopped the seawall built after the

Figure 7.9.   Galveston seawall built after the hurricane of 1900.
COURTESY OF GARY GRIGGS © 2013.

hurricane of 1900. Ike left behind $29.5 billion in losses, making it the third-costliest Atlantic hurricane at the time (see figure 7.10). The backside of the island seemed to be protected but was at a significantly lower elevation than the area immediately behind the seawall, so it suffered major damage from storm surge.

During Superstorm Sandy in 2012, the strength and angle of approach combined to produce a record storm surge in New York City. The water level recorded at Battery Park, at the southern tip of Manhattan, topped 13.9 feet, exceeding the 10.2-foot record set by Hurricane Donna 52 years earlier. The East River (which is not really a river at all but a tidal channel) overflowed its banks, flooding large sections of Lower Manhattan. Seven subway tunnels under the East River were flooded, causing the greatest damage in the 108-year history of the Metropolitan Transportation Authority (see figure 7.11). More than 10 billion gallons of raw and partially treated sewage were released by the

Figure 7.10.   An aerial view of the damage Hurricane Ike inflicted on Gilchrist, Texas, in 2008. House destruction was almost total from storm surge and wind.
COURTESY OF JOCELYN AUGUSTINO, FEMA, VIA WIKIMEDIA COMMONS.

Figure 7.11.   A number of subway and motor-vehicle tunnels in Manhattan were flooded during Superstorm Sandy.
COURTESY OF TIMOTHY KRAUSE CC BY 2.0 VIA FLICKR

storm into the surrounding waters. The storm surge, combined with large waves, caused considerable damage to homes and other buildings, road-ways, boardwalks, and mass-transit facilities in low-lying coastal areas of both New York and New Jersey. Seventy-two people died as a result of Superstorm Sandy, and total damages reached about $50 billion, making it the second-most costly storm in US history, after Katrina.

Damage from Waves

Hurricane-force winds blowing over large expanses of sea surface for several days can generate very large waves. During Superstorm Sandy, a buoy off New York measured a wave 32.5 feet in height, a record for that location, surpassing by more than 6 feet the largest wave generated by Hurricane Irene, which passed through the same area in 2011. Large waves combined with a storm surge will break closer to shore and inten-sify the damage that either might cause alone. Hurricane-driven waves

Figure 7.12. Shoreline damage in Long Beach, New York, from waves and storm surge during Superstorm Sandy in 2012.
COURTESY OF ANDREA BOOHER, FEMA, NATIONAL ARCHIVES.

will scour sand, eroding protective dunes and beaches and leaving only the structures themselves to withstand wave impact. Waves can damage or destroy homes, roads, bridges, and piers. Building codes in some hurricane-prone areas require elevation on pilings or piers, but depending on the depth of embedment into the sand, the amount of beach scour, the storm surge, and wind velocities, even this has not been enough to protect many structures. During Sandy, entire beachfront communities built on the sand in New York and New Jersey were flooded, tipped over, washed inland, or demolished by waves and storm surge (see figure 7.12).

Rainfall and Flooding

Many tend to think of hurricanes, cyclones, and typhoons as primarily coastal hazards, but the intense rainfall that occurs as these disturbances move inland can be even more damaging than coastal impacts. The size of the storm, the speed at which it advances, and the inland topography, vegetation, and land cover influence how much rain falls, over how large an area, how fast it runs off, and potential flood impacts downstream. Where cyclones are large, topography is steep, and these fronts move slowly, rainfall can be very heavy. Where mountains or topographic barriers exist near the coast, precipitation during a large cyclone can be extreme, and many world rainfall records result from these conditions. The island of Reunion in the Indian Ocean is one good example where a record 45 inches of rain fell in just 12 hours; 72 inches, or 6 feet of rain, fell in a single day; and 97 inches, or a little more than 8 feet of precipitation took place in just 2 days—all global records.

Tropical storms don't have to persist as hurricanes to produce significant flooding. In June 1972, Hurricane Agnes (which at the time was the costliest hurricane to hit the United States in recorded history) had deteriorated to a tropical storm by the time it passed over New York and Pennsylvania. The storm covered a circular area with a diameter of about 1,000 miles and generated the greatest rainfall the area had ever recorded. Severe flooding took place in Virginia, Maryland, Pennsylvania, and New York. Maximum precipitation of 19 inches in Pennsylvania forced 100,000 people to flee their homes. Some buildings were submerged under 13 feet of water, and the governor's mansion was flooded. Fifty lives were lost, and damage in Pennsylvania reached $13 billion (in 2019 dollars).

Tropical Storm Allison passed over Houston, Texas, in 2001, and dropped 37 inches of rain in 36 hours, which was 75 percent of the average annual rainfall for the city. Flooding in the fourth-largest city in the nation damaged more than 45,000 homes and businesses. The storm left 41 dead and $13 billion in damage (in 2019 dollars), making it the costliest tropical storm in US history.

Records are made to be broken, however. On August 25, 2017, Hurricane Harvey collided with the coast of Texas with 130-mile-per-hour winds and then pushed inland. The hurricane dropped more than 50 inches of rain on parts of Houston, which was a national record. Damages exceeded $125 billion, and 103 lives were lost (see figure 7.13).

Figure 7.13.   Flooding in Port Arthur, Texas, from Hurricane Harvey in 2017.
COURTESY OF STAFF SERGEANT DANIEL MARTINEZ, SOUTH CAROLINA NATIONAL GUARD, PUBLIC
DOMAIN, VIA WIKIMEDIA COMMONS.

HURRICANE KATRINA

Hurricane Katrina, which hammered the Gulf Coast in late August 2005, was one of the deadliest hurricanes to ever strike a US coast, causing the deaths of 1,833 people; 86 percent of these were from Louisiana, but neighboring Mississippi suffered 238 fatalities. A study of cause of death for nearly 1,000 of these victims revealed that 40 percent were due to drowning, 25 percent resulted from injury and trauma, and 11 percent were caused by heart conditions. Katrina also produced the greatest amount of property damage, at $108 billion, of any recorded storm to hit the coast of the United States. After passing over Florida, where 14 people died, the storm wreaked havoc on Biloxi and Gulfport, Mississippi, then continued west across southeastern Louisiana, with devastating storm surges ranging from 10 to 28 feet above sea level. While there are some who fail to heed hurricane warnings and prefer to have hurricane parties in their beachfront homes, when storm surges reach these levels, neither your party nor your house are going to end well. Hurricane warnings are not to be taken casually.

New Orleans sits in a depressed natural bowl between the Mississippi River levees on one side and the levees around Lake Pontchartrain on the other. One of the challenges of protecting the city is that more than half of it lies on average about 6 feet below sea level. The wetlands and barrier islands also have been shrinking and eroding because of the channelization of the Mississippi River for shipping, so floods don't replenish the sediments as they did under natural conditions. Because of its location in this bowl, once flooded, it takes a very long time to remove the floodwaters and then recover. And with its low elevation and the reduction of much of the original natural protection provided by wetlands and barrier islands from storm surges, New Orleans is extremely vulnerable to hurricanes.

To make matters worse, the city is sinking and has been for decades because of the history of draining wetlands and groundwater extraction, as well as the overall subsidence of the Mississippi Delta from the thousands of feet of accumulated sediment over millions of years. The closest tide gauge to New Orleans at Grand Isle has recorded a rise in sea level of 9.13 millimeters per year, or 3 feet per century, over the past 72 years. This is about 3 times higher than the historic global rise in sea level. To call this a serious problem would be an understatement, and it presents major challenges for this colorful and historic city, challenges that will only be amplified in the future as the level of the oceans continues to rise and the land beneath the city continues to subside.

The combined effects of large waves and the storm surge during Hurricane Katrina led to the collapse of the levees protecting New Orleans (see figure 7.14). Eighty percent of the city was ultimately flooded, displacing more than a million people. The impact on New Orleans was amplified by a combination of poor pre- and posthurricane responses and rescue and recovery efforts at the local, state, and federal levels. An aging and poorly maintained federal system of levees, failure of residents to respond to evacuation warnings, and slow and uncoordinated responses at every level of government all contributed to the disaster and loss of life in New Orleans.

Figure 7.14.   Levee and floodwall failure during Hurricane Katrina in 2005 led to the flooding of New Orleans.
COURTESY OF JERRY BROWN, HOUSING AND URBAN DEVELOPMENT, NATIONAL ARCHIVES.

While warnings are now given by NOAA at the first indication of an approaching hurricane to allow time for residents in potentially affected areas to prepare or evacuate, these storms have minds of their own. Hurricanes frequently change direction prior to making landfall, so it is very difficult to make precise predictions. Hurricane histories are well known, and barrier islands and low-lying areas along the Gulf and Atlantic coasts of the United States have been regularly battered. Death tolls have generally declined due to hurricane-warning systems, while property damages during large storms have risen overall due to a combination of more intense shoreline development and increases in property values. There is a reasonably high probability that future hurricanes will be more intense, which doesn't bode well for communities in hurricane-prone areas. While newer building codes can help reduce damages, with recent events like Katrina, Sandy, Harvey, Irma, and Maria, where total damages reached more than $500 billion (in 2019 dollars), we can really only afford to build strong enough to withstand certain wind velocities and water depths. Though the climate, warm water, and white sandy beaches of the Gulf and southern Atlantic coasts clearly have their appeal, living on the shoreline here has distinct risks.

CHAPTER EIGHT

Tsunamis

I HAVE SPENT ABOUT 12 MONTHS OF MY LIFE ON SHIPS AT SEA THROUGH a combination of oceanographic research vessels in the North Pacific Ocean, the Semester at Sea program, and a few cruise ships. And while I've experienced rough weather during those voyages and cruises, making it challenging on occasion to carry out research or give stand-up lectures, none of these experiences begin to compare with the waves described in this chapter. Whether from massive seafloor earthquakes, volcanic eruptions, huge landslides that cascade quickly into coastal waters, or a nasty combination of storm waves and ocean currents, waves at sea or at the shoreline can become frighteningly large under the right conditions. And regardless of the size of the boat or ship you are on, when you encounter a wave in the 70- to 90-foot range, quite often the wave wins, and the ship loses. This isn't meant to imply that going to sea in a large ship is inherently dangerous but simply to explain that under the right (or wrong) conditions, all bets are off. The great majority of ships at sea never experience these situations, but there are some bizarre examples of boats and ships encountering extreme waves. In striking contrast to the damage these massive waves can inflict on a ship of any size are those encountered by the big-wave surfers described in chapter 3. These adventure seekers go looking for big waves in a drive to conquer the world's largest waves on a 10- or 12-foot-long surfboard.

LITUYA BAY, ALASKA, 1958

On the night of July 9, 1958, a 7.7 magnitude earthquake along the Fairweather Fault in southeast Alaska shook loose about 40 million cubic yards of rock (that's a lot of rocks, roughly 4 million dump-truck loads) high above the northeastern side of Lituya Bay. This huge mass of rock plunged from an elevation of about 3,000 feet down into the bay. The impact of the rock and debris generated a local but colossal tsunami that washed 1,720 feet up the ridge on the opposite side of the inlet.

How could anyone possibly know that the wave was this high? Well, the wave hit with such power that it swept completely over a spur of land, removing all trees and vegetation at elevations as high as 1,720 feet above the level of the bay (see figures 8.1 and 8.2). Thousands of trees

Figure 8.1.   Lituya Bay, Alaska, 1958. The lighter-colored trim line around the edges of the bay shows where the tsunami removed all the trees. Cenotaph Island is in the middle of the bay, and the mountain where the rockslide occurred is at the rear of the bay on the left side.

Figure 8.2. The rockslide into Lituya Bay came from the mountainside on the right side of the photo and washed 1,720 feet up the mountain on the left side, removing all of the trees and soil down to bedrock.
COURTESY OF D. J. MILLER, US GEOLOGICAL SURVEY, PUBLIC DOMAIN, VIA WIKIMEDIA COMMONS; ARROWS ADDED.

were uprooted or broken off and swept away by the wave, the highest ever documented on the planet. For comparison, the Empire State Building with its antenna is 1,470 feet high. A wave this high is not something you want to be in the way of.

This mammoth wave then continued down the 7-mile length of Lituya Bay, ripping out or snapping off trees on either side of the bay at elevations up to 600 feet, and then proceeded to wash over a sand spit at the mouth of the bay and into the Gulf of Alaska. The force of the wave stripped the soil off down to bedrock and broke off large, old spruce trees, some with trunks up to 6 feet in diameter.

There were three unfortunate fishing boats anchored in Lituya Bay on the night the giant wave washed through. For decades, the bay had been a convenient and safe place for boats to anchor overnight or to find some relief from the frequent rough weather offshore. Orville Wagner and his wife, Mickey, were killed when their boat was sunk after being hit by the superwave. Bill and Vivian Swanson, who were asleep in the *Badger*, and Howard Ulrich and his seven-year-old son Junior, in the 38-foot *Edrie*, all survived. Both boats were anchored about a mile up Lituya Bay from the entrance.

Howard Ulrich first reported hearing a deafening boom, like an explosion, at the head of the bay about 2.5 minutes after the earthquake was first felt. The violent motion of the waters from the 7.7 magnitude earthquake woke Howard, who watched the mountains shaking and clouds and dust coming from their peaks. While it was evening, it was also an Alaskan summer, when it stays pretty light all night long. After observing the chaos for perhaps 2 minutes, he noticed a gigantic wall of water coming down the inlet toward them, cutting a swath of trees along both shorelines. He estimated the wave to be 50 to 75 feet high and very steep as it got closer.

Finally realizing that he had to respond, he got a life jacket on his young son and started the engine but was unable to raise the anchor before the wave hit. He had steered the *Edrie* to face the wave directly, and as the boat rose, the anchor chain snapped. The vessel, with Howard and his son, was carried toward and possibly over the south shore by the wave and then back toward the center of the bay by the backwash. The water in the bay swashed back and forth for about 30 minutes and then became calm. After somehow keeping the boat under control throughout this violent ordeal, Howard and Junior Ulrich powered out of Lituya Bay at eleven o'clock that night, missing their anchor but otherwise safe, uninjured, and extremely lucky.

The Swansons were also very fortunate. Based on Bill Swanson's description of the length of time it took the wave to reach his boat after overtopping Cenotaph Island in the middle of the bay, the wave may have been traveling up to 600 miles per hour. The *Badger*, still at anchor, was lifted by the wave and carried completely over the sand spit at the entrance of the bay, stern first and riding the wave like a surfboard but backward. Bill reported looking down at the top of the trees, estimated at about 80 feet tall, as they were carried over the spit. The wave broke, and the boat hit the bottom and began taking on water. The Swansons abandoned their sinking boat, got into a small dingy, and were fortunately rescued by another fishing boat 2 hours later.

This wasn't the first event to generate large waves in Lituya Bay, however. Famous French explorer LaPerouse (who is credited with the discovery of the bay in 1786) in his ship logs commented on the lack of trees and vegetation on the sides of the bay, "as though everything had been cut cleanly like with a razor blade." Other early explorers had also commented on successive lines of cut trees, indicative of other large landslides and inundations.

Photographs of trimlines, where all the trees were removed, show that at least one and possibly two waves occurred between 1854 and 1916. These trimlines were largely destroyed by a huge 1936 wave that uprooted and broke trees off as high as 500 feet around the bay. The 1958 wave, however, removed all the previous evidence and was the largest wave yet. Because of the unique geologic and tectonic conditions of Lituya Bay, such giant waves will undoubtedly occur here again in the future.

LISBON, PORTUGAL, 1755

One of the earliest large tsunamis for which a well-documented record exists followed a series of three very large earthquakes that struck offshore of Portugal's capital city, Lisbon, on the morning of November 1, 1755. Most of the city's residents were in the churches and cathedrals for the All Saints' Day mass. Much of the city was left in ruins within seconds, and soon after, fires began burning through the rubble. Most sources report that the earthquakes killed about 30,000 people, but some believe that the death toll may have been twice as high. Many survivors fled to the wharves of the city's port to escape the fires and falling buildings, only to be met by the first tsunami, which surged up the Tagus River estuary within about an hour (see figure 8.3). This initial wave reached a height of about 40 feet and took another 1,000 lives. This was followed by two more tsunamis that surged into the city.

Figure 8.3. Artist's depiction of the 1755 Lisbon, Portugal, tsunami.
COURTESY OF G. HARTWIG, VOLCANOES AND EARTHQUAKES (1887).

A rather detailed story of the events of that morning along the water-front comes from an account written by Rev. Charles Davy, a survivor:

I heard a general outcry, "The sea is coming in, we shall all be lost." Upon this, turning my eyes towards the river, which in that place is nearly four miles broad, I could perceive it heaving and swelling in the most unaccountable manner, as no wind was stirring. In an instant there appeared, at some small distance, a large body of water, rising as if it were a mountain. It came on foaming and roaring, and rushed towards the shore with such impetuosity, that we all immediately ran for our lives as fast as possible; many were actually swept away, and the rest above their waist in water at a good distance from the banks.

For my own part I had the narrowest escape, and should certainly have been lost, had I not grasped a large beam that lay on the ground, till the water returned to its channel, which it did almost at the same instant, with equal rapidity. As there now appeared at least as much danger from the sea as the land,

and I scarce knew whither to retire for shelter. I took a sudden resolution of returning back, with my clothes all dripping, to the area of St. Paul's. Here I stood some time and observed the ships tumbling and tossing about as in a violent storm; some had broken their cables and were carried to the other side of the Tagus; others were whirled about with incredible swiftness; several large boats were turned keel upwards.

It was at this time of which I am now speaking, that the fine new Quay, built entirely of rough marble, at an immense expense, was entirely swallowed up, with all the people on it, who had fled thither for safety, and had reason to think themselves out of danger in such a place; at the same time, a great number of boats and small vessels, anchored near it (all likewise full of people, who had retired thither for the same purpose), were all swallowed up, as in a whirlpool and nevermore appeared.

The tsunami was even larger at the coastal city of Lagos along the Algarve, the southern coast of Portugal, and may have reached an elevation of 100 feet. The wave continued to spread and went on to damage the ports of Cadiz in Spain, where it was reported to have killed at least one-third of the population. Safi, Agidir, Ceuta, and Mazagon on the coast of Morocco were damaged, as well. The tsunami traveled a considerable distance north, causing some minor damage in Brest at Brittany, some flooding in England in the Scilly Islands and in Cornwall, and extensive flooding in the cities of Cork and Galway in Ireland (Galway is about 1,000 miles from Lisbon). The wave also spread west into the Atlantic, reaching Madeira, where observers recorded a run-up that reached an elevation of 13 feet, as well as the Canary Islands and the Azores, 800 to 900 miles offshore, where most ports were damaged. Total fatalities in Portugal, Spain, and Morocco from the tsunami are believed to be as high as 70,000.

Nearly all the very large global earthquakes recorded since 1900 have taken place around the margins of the Pacific, which are dominated by subduction zones (the impact zones of historic and future large earthquakes and their accompanying tsunamis), where one tectonic plate slides beneath another. These collisions have created a series of deep trenches surrounding the Pacific Basin: the Peru-Chile, Middle America, Aleutian, Kurile, Japan, Philippine, Tonga-Kermadec, and Hikurangi Trenches. The subduction process is not a smooth one, but rather friction between two massive plates allows the descending oceanic plate to drag down the edge of the overlying continental plate. Typically, after several hundred years, the stress overcomes friction. Plates then may slip as much as 10 to 20 feet, which generates very large earthquakes (magnitude 8–9), with the overlying plate rebounding upward and displacing a massive amount of seawater—a tsunami.

With the exception of the Puerto Rico Trench in the Caribbean Sea and the South Sandwich Trench between Antarctica and the tip of South America, the Atlantic Ocean is devoid of trenches and subduction zones. It has a totally different geologic and tectonic history than the Pacific Ocean, which is why the origin of the 1755 Lisbon earthquake and tsunami are still a topic of debate between geologists and seismologists. While there is general agreement that the earthquake took place offshore of the Iberian Peninsula, the exact source has been difficult to pin down, although the present belief is that it occurred on the Azores-Gibraltar fracture zone, an active tectonic boundary between the Eurasian and African plates.

A seafloor survey in 1992 detected a fault with thousands of feet of near-vertical displacement, which may have been the source of the earthquake and the subsequent tsunami. Lisbon also suffered a large earthquake in 1321 and another in 1531, perhaps from the same fault zone. These large shocks were spaced 210 and then 224 years apart. In 1969, a magnitude 7.8 earthquake occurred along the same Azores-Gibraltar fracture zone, leading to 13 deaths and a tsunami just 4 feet in height. This was the largest earthquake to strike Europe since the 1755 event. Interestingly, the time elapsed since that devastating earthquake and tsunami had been 214 years. Is there some regularity here that may provide an indication of when the next event may arrive?

As with many other seismically related hazards, however, a major earthquake and tsunami every several hundred years is a difficult hazard to prepare for. The shoreline from Cape Mendocino in northern California to Vancouver Island, which lies directly onshore from the Cascadia Subduction Zone and is discussed later, is a good example of this dilemma. Can we significantly reduce the losses from a very large magnitude earthquake and tsunami, and where does this lie in our personal and government priorities?

ANCHORAGE, ALASKA, 1964

At 5:36 a.m. local time on March 27, 1964, the second-largest global earthquake of the last century, a 9.2 magnitude shock, occurred in the Prince William Sound area of Alaska as the Pacific Plate lurched northward, underneath the North American Plate. This remains the most powerful earthquake in US history, the second-largest ever recorded, and its shaking lasted 4 to 5 minutes. While many have probably felt an earthquake that lasted 4 or 5 seconds, 4 or 5 minutes of strong shaking must have felt like an eternity.

Although we didn't have the tsunami warning system in place then that exists today, the Honolulu Magnetic and Seismic Observatory issued its first "tidal wave advisory" about an hour and half later. They broadcasted that a tsunami was possible and that it would reach the Hawaiian Islands in about 5 hours. A short while later, after learning about tsunami damage on Kodiak Island, Alaska, the Honolulu Observatory issued a formal "tidal wave/seismic sea-wave warning" announcing that damage was possible in Hawaii and throughout the entire Pacific Basin but without any prediction of the intensity of the tsunami. Our understanding of tsunamis was much more limited at that time, and these events were still being called "tidal waves," even though they have absolutely nothing to do with the tides.

That huge earthquake did generate a deadly tsunami that took 124 lives (106 in Alaska, 13 in California, and 5 in Oregon) and caused about $2.4 billion (in 2019 dollars) in property losses along the Pacific coast of North America from Alaska to southern California, as well as in Hawaii. Waves reached their greatest inland elevation of 220 feet in Alaska, 32 feet in British Columbia, 12 feet in Oregon, about 15 feet in California, and more than 16 feet in Hawaii. Today, however, more than 50 years later, our national and Pacific tsunami warning centers can issue alerts within minutes of a large earthquake, project the potential size of a tsunami for those areas in its likely path, and estimate an arrival time.

In addition to the tsunami produced by the displacement of the sea-floor in the Aleutian Trench in 1964, there were about 20 smaller local tsunamis generated by submarine and subaerial (terrestrial) landslides that were responsible for most of the tsunami damage. Underwater land-slides triggered by the earthquake, some in water more than 1,000 feet deep, sent destructive waves into the Alaskan community of Chenega, where 23 of 75 residents lost their lives and all but one building were destroyed. The local people in Chenega had no time to get to higher ground, which is what signs now posted all along low-lying West Coast communities in Washington, Oregon, and California now warn you to do. Deadly waves hit Chenega just 4 minutes after the earthquake and reached elevations 90 feet above sea level. The only building to survive intact was the schoolhouse, which somewhat fortuitously was built 100 feet above sea level (see figure 8.4). With essentially no warning time,

Figure 8.4. The schoolhouse in Chenega, Alaska, the only building in the village that survived the 1964 tsunami.
COURTESY OF THE US GEOLOGICAL SURVEY.

there was virtually nothing anyone in Chenega could have done, except perhaps be in the schoolhouse or out of town that day.

The town of Whittier, Alaska, was also hit hard by the 1964 tsunami, where water reached more than 100 feet in elevation, destroying two sawmills, the Union Oil tank farm and wharf, the Alaska Railroad depot, and many wood-frame buildings. Of the Whittier population of 70 people, 13 died.

About 3 hours after the earthquake, a tsunami reached Tofino, on the exposed western coast of Vancouver Island, and washed up a fjord to hit Port Alberni twice, destroying 55 homes and damaging 375 others, with total damage in British Columbia reaching $76 million (in 2019 US dollars). Four children were killed on the central Oregon coast at Beverly Beach State Park near the town of Newport.

In Crescent City, the northernmost town in California, just 15 miles south of the Oregon border, 12 people died when the tsunami washed through the harbor and then into the downtown business district (see figures 8.5 and 8.6). This was the most destructive tsunami to batter California's coast in recorded history, and Crescent City was the hardest hit. The series of waves that arrived by the light of a full moon pushed buildings off their foundations and into other structures and swept vehicles and wood-frame structures into the ocean. Wave run-up extended 800 to 2,000 feet inland in the low-lying commercial and residential areas of the city, with water depths of up to 8 feet in city streets and as deep as 13 feet along the shoreline. The largest waves struck the waterfront area at 1:45 a.m., demolishing 150 stores, and littering the streets with huge redwood logs from a nearby sawmill.

The first wave only caused minor flooding of shops and stores near the shoreline. The residents had experienced previous false tsunami alarms, so they weren't all that worried about a foot of water downtown. Gary Clawson and his father owned a tavern called the Longbranch. That evening, they, along with Gary's mother, his fiancée, and two employees, came downtown to look over the tavern, clean up a little, and retrieve the cash box. Then they unfortunately decided to have another drink to celebrate his father's birthday. Gary recalls, "My dad, I'll never forget, jumped on the bar, grabbed a beer and said 'Well happy birthday to me.' And

Figure 8.5. Damage from the 1964 tsunami in Crescent City, California.
COURTESY OF ORVILLE MAGOON © 1964.

Figure 8.6. Mural on the side of a building in Crescent City depicting the effects of the 1964 tsunami, including a map of the city showing areas damaged and destroyed.
COURTESY OF GARY GRIGGS © 2008.

then said, 'Let it come.'" As soon as he said this, rising waters ripped the Longbranch off its foundation. After the group escaped to the floating roof, Clawson found a boat to rescue his family and friends. Sadly, the boat capsized in the rough water, and everyone, except 27-year-old Gary Clawson, drowned. Years later, he was still trying to make sense of what happened that night, as he was spared but the waters killed his parents and fiancée: "I've lived (the 1964 tsunami) 2 or three 3 a week since it happened."

Peggy Coons and her husband, Roxey, were the keepers for the Battery Point Lighthouse in Crescent City at the time (see figure 8.7). They recorded their observations of the fourth, and largest, wave:

The water withdrew as if someone had pulled the plug. It receded a distance of three-quarters of a mile from the shore. We were looking down, as though from a high mountain, into a black

Figure 8.7. The Battery Point Lighthouse in Crescent City.

abyss. It was a mystic labyrinth of caves, canyons, basins and pits, undreamed of in the wildest of fantasies.

The basin was sucked dry. At Citizen's Dock, the large lumber barge was sucked down to the ocean bottom. In the distance, a black wall of water was rapidly building up, evidenced by a flash of white as the edge of the boiling and seething seawater reflected the moonlight.

Then the mammoth wall of water came barreling towards us. It was a terrifying mass, stretching up from the ocean floor and looking much higher than the island [Battery Point where the lighthouse was]. Roxey shouted, "Let's head for the tower!"—but it was too late. "Look out!" he yelled and we both ducked as water struck, split and swirled over both sides of the island. It struck with such force and speed that we felt like we were being carried along with the ocean. It took several minutes before we realized that the island hadn't moved. . . .

Big bundles of lumber were tossed around like matchsticks into the air, while others just floated gracefully away. . . . When the tsunami assaulted the shore, it was like a violent explosion. A thunderous roar mingled with all the confusion. Everywhere we looked, buildings, cars, lumber and boats shifted around like crazy. The whole beachfront moved, changing before our very eyes. . . . The tide turned, sucking everything back with it. Cars and buildings were now moving seaward again. . . . The rest of the night, the water and debris kept surging in and out of the harbor.

There was one positive outcome of that deadly disaster, however. Rather than completely rebuilding the downtown, the city turned an entire strip of oceanfront property about 700 feet wide, where losses were greatest, into grassy parkland (see figure 8.8). It has remained parkland for 57 years now, a permanent buffer for future tsunamis.

SUMATRA, INDONESIA, 2004

The tsunami generated by the magnitude 9.3 Sumatra earthquake the day after Christmas 2004 was responsible for more fatalities than any other

Figure 8.8. A shoreline park has replaced much of the area of Crescent City destroyed by the 1964 Alaskan tsunami.
COURTESY OF KENNETH AND GABRIELLE ADELMAN, CALIFORNIA COASTAL RECORDS PROJECT © 2019.

tsunami in recorded history and affected the coastlines of 14 countries around the Indian Ocean. This was also the second-largest earthquake ever recorded and resulted from the Indian Plate descending beneath the Burma Plate at a subduction zone, a virtually identical geological setting as the 1964 Alaska earthquake. The sudden uplift of the seafloor by 6 to 15 feet as the Burma Plate rebounded upward displaced massive amounts of ocean water that resulted in a tsunami that reached the adjacent Sumatra coastline within 15 to 20 minutes. Waves with heights of more than 30 feet reached maximum elevations of up to 100 feet above sea level and washed about a mile and a half inland, leaving death and destruction along the way. The great majority of the approximately 228,000 deaths were related to the tsunami. Indonesia was the hardest-hit nation (more than 131,000 fatalities), followed by Sri Lanka (35,322 lives lost); India (12,405 fatalities); and Thailand (5,395 deaths). More than 1.5 million people were left homeless (see figure 8.9).

Figure 8.9. A severely damaged home in the coastal area of Banda Aceh, Indonesia, following the 2004 tsunami.
COURTESY OF GUY GELFENBAUM, PACIFIC COASTAL AND MARINE SCIENCE CENTER, US GEOLOGICAL SURVEY.

In Thailand, the southwest coast was the area hardest hit, in particular the resort areas of Phuket, Phi Phi, and Khao-Lak (see figure 8.10). The waves arrived about 2 hours after the earthquake, and observers first noticed the water along the shoreline withdrawing—the trough before the crest arrived. This was followed by the first wave, at about 13 feet high, arriving at 10:30 a.m. local time and then, 2.5 minutes later, a second, larger wave more than 20 feet high. The third and largest wave was reported to have been about 36 feet high. These successive waves destroyed all the shoreline structures, including hotels and other resorts, surprising and drowning many tourists and inhabitants.

About 100 lives were believed saved at one Phuket resort when Tilly Smith, a vacationing schoolgirl from England who had recently studied tsunamis in school, noticed the sea receding, one of the signs of an

Figure 8.10. Damage to the resort area of Phuket, Thailand, from the 2004 tsunami.
COURTESY OF STEPHEN KENNEDY, CC BY 2.0 VIA WIKIMEDIA COMMONS.

impending tsunami. She tried to warn her mother, who didn't pay much attention, but she convinced her father that this was the indication of an approaching tsunami. Her father contacted resort security, who then warned the people on the beach to evacuate. Prior to our understanding of tsunamis, locals in places like Japan or Hawaii, for example, often would walk out across the shoreline exposed by receding water to pick up the stranded fish in uncovered reefs and tide pools without realizing what was coming next. After a number of fatalities under these conditions, locals now usually flee inland at this first sign.

The magnitude and power of the Sumatra tsunami is evidenced by the drowning of people more than 3,000 miles away on the opposite side of the Indian Ocean along the shorelines of Somalia, Tanzania, Yemen, and Kenya. In South Africa, 4,800 miles across the entire Indian Ocean, eight people died due to abnormally high sea levels and the tsunami waves.

Although there was some lag between the earthquake and the tsunami, nearly all the victims were completely surprised, in part because there had been no recent history of tsunamis in the Indian Ocean, and as a result, there was no warning system in place at the time. Combined with the very high population densities along the coastlines and the lack of infrastructure, fatalities were very high. Following the massive loss of life, injuries, and destruction from this tragic event, a tsunami warning system was established in the area and became functional in 2006.

FUKUSHIMA, JAPAN, 2011

On Friday, March 11, 2011, at 2:46 p.m., the first of three sequential disasters struck the northeast coast of Japan. The first was a massive 9.0 magnitude earthquake generated 45 miles offshore when the Pacific Plate slid west beneath the Eurasian Plate along a subduction zone. This was the largest earthquake to hit Japan in recent history and the fourth-most powerful earthquake in the world since modern record keeping began in 1900. (The largest and deadliest earthquake and tsunami to strike this century was the 2004 magnitude 9.1 Sumatra event described earlier.) By any measure, this was a massive earthquake with very large consequences (see figure 8.11).

The seafloor displacement of 20 to 25 feet at the offshore trench created an enormous tsunami, which reached the coastline of Japan's northern islands in less than an hour. This was disaster number 2. These waves reached elevations of up to 128 feet above sea level and moved inland as far as 6 miles, flooding more than 200 square miles of low-lying coastal land. The earthquake and tsunami led to the deaths of an estimated 20,000 people, mostly from drowning.

The 2011 Japan tsunami spread out across the Pacific and damaged coastal areas from Alaska to Chile. Waves began to hit the California coast about 10 hours later and were most damaging where the tsunami was funneled into coastal harbors, specifically Crescent City (again) and Santa Cruz, raising water levels, battering boats, and damaging floating docks (see figure 8.12).

Although four Japanese nuclear power plants were automatically shut down following the earthquake, the reactors still required cool-

Figure 8.11. Damage in Yamada Town, Japan, from the 2011 tsunami.
COURTESY OF KATHERINE MUELLER, INTERNATIONAL FEDERATION OF RED CROSS AND RED CRES-
CENT.

Figure 8.12. The 2011 Japan tsunami damaged boats and docks in the Santa
Cruz, California, harbor, 5,000 miles away.
COURTESY OF THE SANTA CRUZ PORT DISTRICT.

ing water to remove large amounts of heat. At the Fukushima Daiichi nuclear plant, tsunami waves overtopped a 33-foot-high seawall protecting the diesel-fueled backup cooling facility, flooding and disabling the system. The loss of cooling water led to three large explosions, followed by nuclear meltdowns at three of the plant's six reactors. Radioactivity was released from the reactor containment vessels due to uncontrolled leakage but also from deliberate venting to the atmosphere to reduce pressure and from deliberate discharge of coolant water to the adjacent ocean. This started disaster number 3.

The approximately 440 tons per day (about 330,000 gallons) of cooling water that was pumped into the reactors combined with an estimated additional 300 tons (a little over 224,000 gallons) of groundwater per day flowing beneath the reactors picked up radiation and carried it to the adjacent ocean. Over the subsequent months, more than 1,000 large tanks were set up to collect the contaminated water. Treatment facilities were constructed to partially clean the water.

This is a complicated story, which is still underway 10 years later. One troubling problem was how to cut off the subsurface flow of groundwater beneath the plant, which was mixing with radioactive water leaking from the reactors and then flowing toward the ocean. The plan finally developed, nearly 3 years after the earthquake, tsunami, and meltdown, included freezing the ground and groundwater beneath the site and building an ice dam to contain the flow. This complex project cost roughly $300 million and is now operational. Hundreds of pipes pump coolant nearly 100 feet into the subsurface to form a mile-long containment wall, attempting to keep additional groundwater from flowing under the reactors. As of 2019, over the 3 years of the ice dam's operation, it had reduced the amount of polluted water by just one-quarter. There is still a long way to go to solve the problems and radioactive pollution generated by the 2011 tsunami.

The greatest amount of radiation (primarily cesium and iodine) entered the ocean off Japan in the first few months after the reactor failures. It was described as the greatest individual emission of artificial radiation into the sea ever reported. In a survey of 170 different types of fish caught off Japan, 42 species tested in the months immediately following the accident had too much radiation for consumption. Water samples were collected regularly by a scientist from Woods Hole Oceanographic Institution across the Pacific and tested for radioactivity. Transit took about 4 years to make the 5,000- to 6,000-mile trip across the Pacific, during which time the cesium-134 could decay and dissipate. Levels of cesium off the West Coast of North America were recorded at less than 1/500 of US government drinking-water standards.

CASCADIA SUBDUCTION ZONE, NORTHWEST COAST OF THE UNITED STATES, 1700

A little more than 320 years ago, on the evening of January 27, 1700, a series of large waves suddenly inundated the east coast of Japan. The arrival and impacts were meticulously recorded at a Buddhist monastery, as were many events throughout Japan's long history, but were a mystery at the time. While tsunamis weren't new to the coast of Japan, in this case there was no nearby earthquake preceding the arrival of the tsunami, which was the expected pattern. The word *tsunami* is a combination of two Japanese words: *tsu*, meaning harbor or port, and *nami* for wave.

The monastery records were literally buried for almost 3 centuries until Brian Atwater, a geologist with the US Geological Survey who was doing fieldwork along the coasts of Oregon and Washington, discovered evidence that the coastal area had subsided many years before, killing vegetation from submergence in saltwater. Ghost forests, consisting of Sitka spruce and red cedar trees, were exposed in backwater estuarine areas, and stumps were still preserved along the shoreline and visible at low tides along the shoreline in some areas (see figure 8.13). These trees and stumps were dated using dendrochronology, or the close examination of their annual growth rings. This careful analysis indicated that the trees had died between 1699 and 1700.

Detailed study of sediments preserved in a number of estuaries and tidal inlets along the Pacific Northwest coast of the United States over the past several decades revealed buried marsh vegetation covered with layers of clean beach sand, which seemed oddly out of place in these muddy, estuarine environments. Dating of these deposits matched with the tree-ring data and was consistent with oral histories about native

Figure 8.13. The ghost forest from the 1700 tsunami along the Oregon coast is exposed at low tide.
COURTESY OF BRIAN ATWATER, US GEOLOGICAL SURVEY.

people living in the coastal area at the time, who referenced severe shaking of the ground and flooding. The ghost forests, the buried vegetation and sediment record, the oral histories of native peoples of the Pacific Northwest, and the ancient tsunami in Japan (now known as the "Orphan Tsunami" because there was no local parent earthquake) all point to a very large earthquake and tsunami in January 1700, which took place on the underlying Cascadia Subduction Zone. This subduction zone extends from Cape Mendocino in northern California to Vancouver Island, a distance of about 550 miles (see figure 8.14). The plate motion and earthquake led to the subsidence of the coastline, drowning trees and marsh vegetation, which was followed by the tsunami that transported

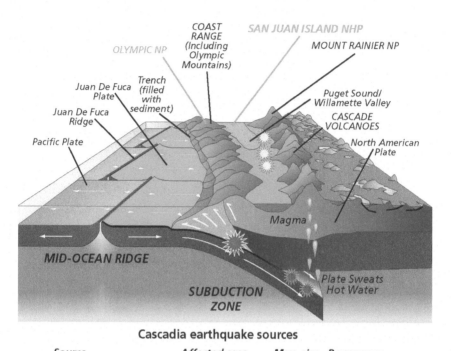

Cascadia earthquake sources

	Source	Affected area	Max. size	Recurrence
	Subduction Zone	West. WA, OR, CA	M 9	500-600 years *(1700)*
	Deep Juan De Fuca Plate	West. WA, OR	M 7+	30-50 years *(1949, 1965, 2001)*
	Crustal faults	WA, OR, CA	M 7+	hundreds of years? *(CE 900, 1872)*

Figure 8.14. The Cascadia Subduction Zone extends from Cape Mendocino in northern California to Vancouver Island.

COURTESY OF R. J. LILLE AND THE NATIONAL PARK SERVICE.

sand from the ocean beaches inland more than a mile and a half along tidal channels, covering low-lying marsh areas.

More than 50 years ago, while a graduate student in oceanography at Oregon State University, I was investigating a deep-sea channel that began not far off the mouth of the Columbia River and extended for more than 1,000 miles along the ocean floor. We were coring sediments from the floor of that channel in water more than 10,000 feet deep. The sediments first collected more than a half-century ago contained the history of great earthquakes. These large-magnitude tremors disturbed the accumulated sediments perched offshore on the continental slope, which flowed downslope as turbidity currents or submarine mudflows, leaving the sandy and muddy deposits behind on the deep-sea floor as a record of these massive events. These sediments preserved the history of at least 19 such massive events over the past 10,000 years—very large, likely magnitude 9 earthquakes, followed by large tsunamis, about every 350 to 500 years.

Today, coastal communities from Vancouver Island to southern California, a distance of well over 1,000 miles, have now become aware of their future tsunami risks through this relatively recent paleotsunami research, or the investigation of the geologic record of ancient tsunamis. The research methods pioneered here are now being employed in other subduction zone settings around the world. If we can recognize and date prehistoric tsunami deposits and their inland extent and depths of flooding, determine the average recurrence intervals between these large events, and figure out how much time has elapsed since the last major event, then we have the ability to more accurately assess which areas are at the highest risks of future catastrophic events and how often or how soon (see figure 8.15). It's not simple but doable where the sediment or vegetation records have been preserved and can be identified and carefully analyzed. While we have never been able to develop a reliable method of predicting precisely when and where a large earthquake is going to occur, this recent research can at least give us a better picture of what is likely to happen with a large tsunami and which areas have the highest probability of a large earthquake in the near future.

Along the US West Coast, these paleotsunami records have led to the posting of tsunami warning signs along low-lying, vulnerable sections of coastlines of all three western states. These signs warn people to evacuate or head quickly to higher ground if a large earthquake occurs or if they are otherwise notified. There has been moderate damage to many small ports and harbors along the Oregon and California coasts from tsunamis over the past century from the Aleutian Trench, such as occurred in 1946 and 1964. Crescent City, on the northern California coast, and

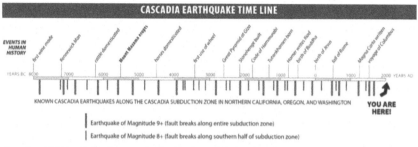

Figure 8.15. A timeline of great Cascadia earthquakes.
COURTESY OF THE OREGON DEPARTMENT OF GEOLOGY AND MINERAL INSTITUTES.

the Santa Cruz Harbor on the central coast are two areas with a record of historic tsunami damage. Identifying those areas that tsunamis have affected in the past and determining their inland extent and elevation is important for planning for potential future inundation and reducing damage and loss of life.

While the passage of time can begin to erase the memory of fatalities and destruction from earlier events, we need to accept the reality that plate motion, subduction-zone earthquakes, and tsunamis are a fact of life in certain geographic regions. We know where these regions are and that these events will occur again. It is our collective responsibility to delineate and mark the areas of historic inundation, post the warning and evacuation signs, and ensure that our alert systems are in place and working. One very large societal challenge, however, is how to prepare and how much to invest in planning for an event that may occur only every 350 to 500 years. We also need to keep in mind that the last Cascadia earthquake and tsunami took place 320 years ago. It could happen tomorrow but might not happen for another 50 or 100 years or more.

With so many other things to worry about, do we need to get stressed out about tsunamis in California? For me, it's not on my list of top 10 concerns. Your odds of dying in a tsunami in California are far lower than virtually any other risk we all face daily: commuting to work, bicycling, or motorcycling on a busy highway—even being bitten by a dog. Over the past 200 years, there have been just 17 deaths from the six tsunamis large enough to cause significant damage along the coast of California. That's an average of about one life lost every 10 years and lower than virtually any other risk you could imagine. You could still do something dumb, and one person did die on the northern California coast from the 2011 Japan tsunami by standing along the shoreline to take photographs of the incoming wave.

In contrast, however, the 2004 Sumatra earthquake and tsunami took about 228,000 lives, and the 2011 Japanese earthquake and tsunami led to about 20,000 fatalities. The geologic setting of the coastline between Cape Mendocino and Puget Sound is very similar to Japan and Sumatra, being directly onshore from a tsunami source, with just a few precious minutes between a large earthquake and the tsunami arrival at the shoreline. For central and southern California, there would be an hour or two of warning, as this area is not in the direct path of a tsunami from the Cascadia Subduction Zone.

Tsunamis, like earthquakes and hurricanes, are completely beyond human control and can produce widespread death and destruction along developed and populated coastlines. The word *tsunami* generates an emotional response, much like *earthquake* and *shark*. It's just one of those scary things we never want to experience. The approximately 228,000 people who died the day after Christmas in 2004 from the Indian Ocean tsunami serve as a cruel reminder of the forces that lurk offshore around the edges of the Indian and Pacific Oceans.

While most tsunamis result from subduction-zone earthquakes in deep trenches, where one massive tectonic plate slides beneath another, they can also occur where oceanic volcanoes erupt catastrophically or where large landslides run down steep slopes into bodies of water as at Lituya Bay, Alaska. The biggest tsunamis that have ever occurred were likely generated by the impacts of asteroids in the ocean, but no large ones have struck the planet since humans have been on the scene.

The roughly 6-mile-wide asteroid that smashed into the Gulf of Mexico 66 million years ago, likely leading to the demise of the dinosaurs, was traveling at about 45,000 miles per hour and created waves probably more than 1,000 feet high. These waves likely swept inland to the midcontinental United States as far as South Dakota, roughly 1,600 miles away. No worries, though; asteroid impacts 1/100 that size hit Earth only once in a million years on average. While its impact would be enormous, the probability of such an event is very low.

CHAPTER NINE

Some Final Perspectives on the Dangers along the Coast and in the Ocean

VIRTUALLY ANYTHING WE DO EVERY DAY HAS SOME RISK ATTACHED TO it. Many of these activities we don't even give a second thought to: walking across town to see a friend, enjoying a nice long bike ride, or taking a Sunday drive. Yet in the United States, about 700 people die each year from bicycle accidents; 5,000 pedestrians lose their lives; and motor vehicle accidents lead to 35,000 to 40,000 fatalities.

I think that most people worry far more about natural disasters that we have absolutely no control over (tsunamis or hurricanes) or those animals that strike fear into our hearts (sharks, for example) than the seemingly mundane activities we engage in every day. Without question, there are risks along the shoreline and out in the ocean, and the preceding chapters help put these into some perspective relative to the things that fill our everyday lives. These chapters also provide some science and perhaps answer some questions you may have had about dangers of the ocean.

The risks from large-scale natural hazards are closely related to where we live and the structures we live in. The Gulf and South Atlantic coasts of the United States attract hurricanes like magnets, and we have a long and well-documented history of the destruction and fatalities they have left behind. Similar events affect the nations of Southeast Asia and the northern Indian Ocean, where population densities and fatalities are considerably higher. Here they are referred to as typhoons and cyclones.

For millions of people who live where population densities are very high, they have no other choices regarding where they can live and work.

With a warming ocean, it appears that hurricanes, cyclones, and typhoons are becoming more frequent each year, which might give us pause to think about our changing odds regarding our personal safety and our homes. Fortunately, we now have hurricane-tracking and -warning systems in place that provide us a reasonable forecast of approximately where and when a tropical storm or hurricane will make landfall, along with evacuation warnings. Although we can't easily move our homes, we can save our lives.

While tsunamis have been devasting throughout recorded history, the major impacts have not been along US coastlines, with the exception of Alaska and Hawaii, although the Cascadia Subduction Zone, extending about 550 miles from northern California to Vancouver Island, will likely rupture with a very large earthquake accompanied by a major tsunami in the not-too-distant future. Large tsunamis along the West Coast are a much rarer phenomenon than hurricanes along the Gulf and South Atlantic coasts of the United States. In California's roughly 200 years of recorded history, there have been just 17 tsunami deaths—1 fatality every 12 years on average. Almost anything you do in your everyday life in California is more dangerous than a tsunami. However, the approximately 20,000 lives lost in the 2011 earthquake and tsunami in Japan and the nearly 228,000 fatalities from the 2004 Indian Ocean tsunami paint a very different picture of risk in these areas.

There are lots of potentially dangerous creatures in the coastal ocean, but none of them have any animosity toward humans. With some awareness of where we enter the water and what sorts of potentially harmful animals are around, we can avoid fatal encounters. While sharks fall into a somewhat different category because they do on occasion attack people, the odds are exceedingly low of being attacked or dying from a shark. While the rare attacks are widely covered in the media, the risk of a shark attack is almost infinitely low relative to driving to the beach. Nearly 900 people drown every day on average in the waters of the world, with 10 of these being in the United States. During the peak of the pandemic, about

14,000 people every day on the planet were dying from COVID-19, with about 4,000 lives lost in the United States on the worst days.

Many of the lives lost along the shoreline or in shallow water are a result of simply not being careful, not being aware of surroundings or making bad decisions. Rip currents, large surf, sneaker waves are all common, and while these words don't have the verbal impact of *hurricane* or *shark*, they generally present far greater risks to the average beach visitor. The 10 lives lost along the northern California shoreline during 4 weeks of the 2020–2021 winter are sad testimony to this reality. These individuals, young and old, alone or with families, were carried fully clothed from solid ground into the cold pounding winter surf within seconds, where chances of survival were very low in all cases.

The beach and the ocean provide countless benefits, and tens of millions of annual beachgoers, residents, visitors, and those involved in other ocean activities provide ample evidence of this attraction. There are natural hazards that are well beyond our control and that do present threats if we are in the wrong place at the wrong time, but we can make conscious decisions in most cases for reducing these risks. Similarly, while there are a number of sea creatures that use venom or teeth for protection or for stunning or capturing prey, the odds of encounters can be greatly reduced with caution and awareness of where we are swimming and not approaching or provoking these animals. Then there are those shoreline hazards, all related to ocean waves, that are perhaps among the most dangerous of all, simply because we don't generally realize what can happen in a few seconds when we turn our backs on the ocean or aren't aware of our surroundings.

All in all, the ocean and the beach are natural resources that we should enjoy, where we can relax, experience, explore, or be alone with nature, with special people, or with our thoughts. This book is not intended to frighten you away from enjoying these pleasures or experiences but rather to provide some perspective and hopefully some useful information about potentially dangerous activities and how to avoid or reduce risks.

INDEX

63, 63–64; dangerous, 43–44, 67; flower urchins, 59–60, *60*; great white sharks, 44–47, *45*; Humboldt squid, 52; IUCN for, 61; lionfish, 56–59, *57*; psychology of, x; risk from, 1–5, *3*; saltwater crocodiles, *48*, 48–50; sea snakes, 65, *66*, 67; sea urchins, 59–60, *61*; sharks, ix, 1–5, *3*, 44–47, *45*, 150, 154–55; shrimp, 55; snails, *63*, 63–64; stingrays, 43, 60–62, *62*; stonefish, 52–54, *53*; striped tiger shark, 46; while scuba diving, 35, *36*

seafloors: displacement of, 142; research on, 147–48; technology for, *25*, 132

sea ice, 83–84

sea snakes, 65, *66*, 67

sea urchins, 59–60, *61*

sexual dimorphism, 48–49

sharks, ix, 1–5, *3*, 44–47, *45*, 150, 154–55

Shedd, John August, 81

ships: *Badger*, 128–29; Bermuda Triangle for, 94–97, *95–96*, 101–2; *Bremen*, 75, 80; *Caledonian Star*, 75, 80; *Conception*, 89–91, *90*; container, 76–77, *76–77*; cruise, 75–77; *Cyclops*, 94–96, *95*; dive boats, 89–91, *90*; *Edrie*, 128; *Gaines Mills*, 101; history of, 69–73, *70–72*; *Holoholo*, 77–79; *Marine Sulpher Queen*, 96, 96–97; *München*, 76–77, *76–77*; *Nereus*, 95; *Norwegian Dawn*, 75–76; for oceanographers, 74–81, *75–77*, *80*; *Prinsendam*, 76, 87, *88*, 89; *Proteus*, 95; *Queen Elizabeth*, 70, 73; *Queen Elizabeth II*, 75; *Queen Mary*, 70–73, *72*; risk for, 81–87, *82–83*, *85*, *87–88*, 89–91, *90*; *Spray*, 69–70, *70*; *Titanic*, *82–83*, 82–85; tsunamis for, 125; *Universe*, 85, *85*, 103–4; *Universe Explorer*, 85; *Williamsburgh*, 87, 89; *World Glory*, 74–75, *75*. See also rogue waves

shock, 50

shrimp, 55, 62

skin cancer, 7

sleeper waves. *See* sneaker waves

Slocum, Joshua, 69–70, *70*

Smith, Russell, *24*

Smith, Tilly, 140–41

snails, *63*, 63–64

snakes, 65, *66*, 67

sneaker waves, 14–16, *16–17*, 18

snorkeling, 52–53

Solomon Islands, 48

Somalia, 141

South Africa, 51, 63, 67, 141

South Sandwich Trench, 132

Spain, 41, 131